W9-BND-730

SINO-SOVIET RIVALRY

IMPLICATIONS FOR U.S. POLICY

Edited by

CLEMENT J. ZABLOCKI

Published for

THE CENTER FOR STRATEGIC STUDIES
GEORGETOWN UNIVERSITY

by

FREDERICK A. PRAEGER, *Publishers*
New York • Washington • London

FREDERICK A. PRAEGER, *Publishers*
111 Fourth Avenue, New York, N.Y. 10003, U.S.A.
77-79 Charlotte Street, London W.1, England

Published in the United States of America in 1966
by Frederick A. Praeger, Inc., Publishers

Library of Congress Catalog Card Number: 66-26555

Printed in the United States of America

ACKNOWLEDGMENTS

In a very real sense, this book is the work of many hands. As the manuscript was being prepared, it became increasingly evident to me how helpful so many individuals had been and how much their work contributed to this effort.

I am deeply grateful to the experts and specialists whose articles make up the bulk of this volume. There would have been no book had not their original statements before the House Foreign Affairs Subcommittee on the Far East and Pacific been of such high quality. For the unanimous and unfailing courtesy and cooperation of those who testified and then contributed to this book, I am deeply appreciative. Also I am very grateful indeed to the additional contributors.

A special debt of gratitude must be acknowledged to Admiral Arleigh Burke, Director of the Center for Strategic Studies at Georgetown University. It was he who first suggested the publication of a book upon the Sino-Soviet conflict hearings and offered the assistance of the Center in bringing the project to fruition. The help which has been received from the Center's excellent staff, including its Executive Secretary, Dr. David M. Abshire, Mr. Richard V. Allen, Dr. Cornelius D. Sullivan, and Miss Mary Catherine McCarthy, has been invaluable.

In the initial stages of the editing work, I was fortunate to have the assistance of Dr. Alvin J. Cottrell, who helped plan the organization of the book, and Mr. Kenneth Gilmore, who gave editorial advice and guidance. In the later stages, much of the burden of coordinating the work with the contributors, with the Center and with the publisher fell to Mrs. Robin de Campi. The work of Mrs. de Campi, who also did detailed editing, was most essential to the final publication.

Acknowledgements are due also to Mr. Harry Cromer, Mr. Marian Czarnecki, Miss June Nigh, and Mrs. Doris McCracken of the House Foreign Affairs Committee staff and to Jack Sullivan of my Congressional staff for their help.

C. J. Z.

Preface

—*CLEMENT J. ZABLOCKI*

DURING THE YEARS WHEN MANY OF US GREW UP, THE WORLD ORDER seemed as permanent and secure as the arrangement of colors and lines and names on every classroom globe. There was a place for everything and everything was in its place—or appeared to be. In those days world history seemed to stand still: the sun had never set on the British Empire, the French Army was the mightiest in the world, and the United States still heeded the admonition of George Washington to avoid entangling alliances.

In 1939, however, World War II began and the world order crumbled. When the war was over, many of us believed that the map would be restored to its prewar appearance. But we soon found that the original order couldn't be put back together again.

Attempts to pick up the pieces had little success. Powerful forces were at work to thwart the restoration of the *status quo ante bellum*. The sun had set on the British Empire, the French Army no longer inspired awe, and the United States was entangled in alliances from Ankara to Zeeland.

Almost without exception postwar alliances were aimed at stopping the rapid expansion of Communist power. The end of World War II found Soviet troops in control of almost every part of Eastern and Central Europe. One by one Communist puppet governments were established and nations slipped into the Soviet orbit, among them: Bulgaria, Rumania, Hungary, Poland, Albania, Czechoslovakia, and the eastern part of Germany. Soviet communism was supreme from the Adriatic to the Baltic. Once again Western Europe was in peril.

In Asia too the Communists were at work. Soon they controlled Outer Mongolia, North Korea, and—in time—the mainland of China. By the early 1950s the world resembled two armed camps. On one side were the Western democracies, with their allies in Latin America and the Far East. In this bloc, the United States was the pre-eminent power, providing the massive military and economic help necessary to sustain the free world. On the other side was the Communist bloc, with the Soviet Union at its center and China as a major partner.

Throughout the 1950s the world order seemed as inflexible as it had prior to World War II. The lines that had been drawn, the bonds that had been tied, took on the look of permanence. Some observers were predicting that the East-West confrontation might last generations, perhaps even a century. It would last that long, that is, if a nuclear holocaust did not end it.

During those years we looked upon the Communist world as a monolithic structure—and with reason. The Marxist ideology was clear about the solidarity of all people under communism. This was an "ism" which claimed to strike down barriers of nationality, race, and economic class. The Communist bloc, of course, trumpeted its singleness of purpose, its identity of spirit, and its harmony of cooperation. We knew, of course, that much of the unity was possible only because of the preeminent military power of the USSR in its sphere.

It was difficult, however, to be unimpressed by the cooperation between the Soviet Union and Red China under the aegis of communism. These two nations had been ancient rivals with the longest unsettled border in the world between them.

Yet in the 1950s they were cooperating in an unprecedented manner. The Soviet Union tried to help China become a major world power, complete with nuclear capability. Unity and accord seemed to reign between the two Communist powers. The Sino-Soviet axis, comprising more than a billion people, seemed clearly to represent a grave threat to the security and stability of the free world.

Yet beneath the façade of unity during the 1950s, there were growing fissures and frictions between the USSR and China. Indeed, it is clear in retrospect that the Soviet and Chinese Communists had never appeared to enjoy more harmonious relations. The first clear sign of the seriousness of these mutual antagonisms occurred in early 1960 with the publication of articles on each side attacking the positions and attitudes of the other. The verbal attacks were followed in August 1960 by the withdrawal from China of Soviet technicians—including those assisting with the atomic energy program.

The Western World looked on incredulously, scarcely daring to believe what seemed to be happening. What we were witnessing, we now know, was the beginning of a great schism. The Communist monolith was breaking in two, split between Moscow and Peking. The world order which had seemed relatively permanent only a few years before was breaking up again, and the 1960s thus marked another era of transition.

The Sino-Soviet dispute, once in the open, intensified rapidly. By 1964 there were a multitude of reports about border clashes between the two powers. The polemic between Khrushchev and Mao Tse-tung was virulent and antagonistic. Some observers believe that Khrushchev had decided to break off relations with China, and that this determination led to his removal from office in October 1964 by the Soviet Presidium.

But if the new masters of the Kremlin, Leonid Brezhnev, Alexei Kosygin, and the others, hoped that Sino-Soviet differences could be mended, they were sadly disappointed. Although Chou En-lai visited Moscow in November 1964, it was soon apparent that the basic differences between the two major Communist powers had not been resolved. In the months that followed, Peking resumed the attack. The new Soviet hierarchy displayed considerably more restraint than had Khruschev. There was no evidence, however, that the USSR was in any way capitulating to Peking's demands.

The Sino-Soviet conflict holds a key place in recent world history. It illustrates the proposition that the only constant element of our times is change and the corollary that the only thing predictable about current world politics is the inevitability of the unpredictable.

Who, for example, foresaw that one day the Chinese would picket the Soviet Embassy in Peking, protesting Soviet police treatment of Chinese students attacking the American Embassy in Moscow? Who would have suggested in 1957 that one day the Soviet Union would be building factories in India to provide Delhi with jet fighters to be used in combat against Red China? These are incidents in a world scence more complicated than that of the 1930s, 1940s, and 1950s.

The Sino-Soviet split has introduced a significant factor into the equations of foreign policy. Few decisions in international relations can be made by the United States without some degree of reference to the conflict. It was in this setting that the House Foreign Affairs Subcommittee on the Far East and Pacific, of which I am chairman, determined to hold a series of hearings on the Sino-Soviet Conflict. The purpose of these hearings was to put together various points of view on the Sino-Soviet dispute—its causes, effects, implications for U.S. policy, and prospects for settlement.

Even at the Congressional level there was little information on the Sino-Soviet conflict. There also appeared to be a serious lack of public understanding of the impact of the conflict on world politics. Further, it was clear that the situation posed temptations to indulge in wishful thinking. The desire for a permanent split, and the hope that it would serve the United States and the free world, must not be allowed to lead to false assumptions. Foreign policy at best is full of uncertainties; to construct it on hopes and dreams is to court disaster.

It was the belief of the subcommittee that through hearings the Sino-Soviet conflict could be brought into clearer focus for Members of Congress, who shape and vote on legislation affecting East-West relations. We also wished to provide a meaningful analysis of the dispute for the general public.

There was much to be learned about the Sino-Soviet split and its implications for the rest of the world. The subcommittee sought to find the cause of the split and its principal issues. It was necessary to discover the effect of the dispute on the international Communist movement and on the domestic and foreign policies of the antagonists. Extremely important was learning how the split affected Communist penetration in Latin America and Africa. We wanted to know its impact on Eastern Europe and its effect on the United States position in Asia and elsewhere. We also wanted to know the prospects for resolving the dispute, the implications for United States policy either in the resolution or in the intensification of hostility, and the long-term international effects of the conflict.

We could not, of course, hope to get precise answers to many of these questions. The answers are history yet unrevealed. It was possible, however, to get the opinions and judgments of men who have devoted many years to the study of communism. Their knowledge and insight could be, the subcommittee believed, of inestimable value. By the time the final witness had testified, it was clear that our belief was justified. A wealth of material on the Sino-Soviet conflict had been received, both in formal statements from the witnesses and in the replies of these experts to questions from Members of Congress. This material was the basis for the subcommittee *Report on The Sino-Soviet Conflict and its Implications.*

Despite the wide circulation of the committee report, I was not satisfied that the important data on the Sino-Soviet conflict and its implications for U.S. policy had been communicated to the American public. Press coverage of the hearings had been gratifying, but a complex subject like the Sino-Soviet conflict cannot be treated adequately in a few daily columns of type. I feared that many interested Americans would never have the opportunity to read the report.

Fortunately, The Center for Strategic Studies at Georgetown University was similarly impressed with the results of the hearings. It was suggested that the testimony of the witnesses might be an excellent starting point for a new book on the schism in the Communist world and its effect on U.S. policy. Further, it became evident as the work was in progress that some aspects of the Sino-Soviet conflict had not been treated as fully as they might have been. To achieve a complete and balanced presentation, new material and chapters have been provided by some of those who had testified and also by specialists from The Center for Strategic Studies and the House Foreign Affairs Committee, bringing the number of contributors to twenty-two. In addition, I have included comments of my own to point up the pertinency of the discussion to events that are making headlines the world over.

In these pages the reader will be confronted with conflicting views and speculations as well as parallel ideas. Some fascinating questions are raised: Did the Soviet Union plan to invade China in 1963 to stop the first Chinese nuclear test, as Richard Lowenthal suggests? Is continued U.S. participation in the Vietnam war endangering a continued détente with the Soviet Union, as the reader might infer from the chapter by Ambassador Kennan? From which of the contestants in the Sino-Soviet dispute has the United States more to fear? What is the impact of the dispute on the "Third World"—the uncommitted nations of Latin America, Africa, and Asia? How has the split affected the internal organization of Communist parties throughout the world?

What do the answers to these and other questions imply for United States policy?

Perhaps the reader will ask questions not raised in this book; he will certainly be better able to judge the significance of incidents and trends throughout the world after considering the judgments and opinions of thoughtful observers of the world today.

Table of Contents

Part Three

IMPLICATIONS FOR U.S. POLICY

PART ONE

THE SINO-SOVIET SPLIT

Introduction

EXACTLY WHEN DID THE GREAT SCHISM BETWEEN RUSSIA AND RED CHINA BEGIN? Few authorities are willing to pick one date; in fact there was probably no specific starting point, only a smoldering between the two Communist powers. The first three chapters in Part I treat the conflicts and irritations that caused this smoldering and show how it finally flared open. The next three chapters suggest some of the ramifications of the split for the domestic and foreign policies of the two antagonists. The authors are men who during the late fifties constantly watched and studied the wisps of smoke that occasionally arose from the Communist world, indicating a mounting friction between communism's two titans.

There is a science to studying and interpreting what the Communists say and do. They have their own oblique jargon, and often it is only experts who see the significance of a statement or a seemingly innocent action behind the iron and bamboo curtains. Certainly that is how early signs of the Sino-Soviet dispute were detected—by careful, astute observations of bits and pieces of Communist activity in Russia, China, and Eastern Europe. For example, in the fall of 1958 the Soviet ambassador to Peking returned to his post after an absence of several months. On November 20, the anniversary of the Soviet revolution, he delivered a speech. In Washington, London, New York, and Berlin, the experts studied the text and were alerted. The laborious Marxist wordage contained an unmistakable though subtle attack upon China's claims that its society and economy were swiftly advancing through the commune system.

Subsequently at study centers in the U.S. and abroad, in and out of government, experts on Communist affairs searched for the meaning of Sino-Soviet differences. Were they merely dialogues between Communist theoreticians? Was this an argument over the best practical strategy for the conquest of the free world? Or did the signs of friction signify a sizable power struggle for leadership of the international Communist movement?

Even today the answers to these questions vary. Many experts believe, however, that a first major sign of full-scale dispute occurred in April 1960 on Lenin's birthday. An editorial appeared in the Chinese publication *Red Flag*. Entitled "Long Live Leninism," it criticized Soviet leadership for veering from the true principles of communism as espoused by Lenin.

I recall attending intelligence briefings to learn details of this attack upon the Soviet Union by its Chinese "comrades." But even then there was no certainty as to the size of the split or its implications. I had just returned from serving as a delegate to the United Nations and had filed a lengthy report to Congress on the many kinds of Soviet obstruction to the useful functioning of the U.N. Nikita Khrushchev was at the peak of his power and ambition. It was hard for many to believe that the Chinese would seriously attempt to take him on. In the Communist world, however, the expected can never be counted on.

It was most fortunate, it seems to me, that our subcommittee hearings on the Sino-Soviet conflict—upon which this book is based—were held in March 1965. For the events of that month were of outstanding significance in the continuing chronicle of the Sino-Soviet conflict. On March 1 the long-planned "consultative" meeting of Communist parties was convened in Moscow. In a sense, it was the last gasp of Khrushchevian policy toward Peking (for it was the fallen party chairman who first had called for a party conference) and the beginning of the new regime's efforts to reestablish unity in the Communist movement. March also marked the full-blown resumption of Peking's polemic against the Soviet leadership after a period of relative quiet following the fall of Khrushchev. It became ever more clear that the issues dividing the two Communist powers were deep ones and would not vanish with the changes in the Kremlin.

The intensity of the conflict was demonstrated in a dramatic way by an incident that occurred only several days before the hearings began. China's ambassador to Moscow, Pan Tzu-li, presented a remarkable note of protest from his government to Soviet Foreign Minister Andrei A. Gromyko. It was immediately rejected by Gromyko.

The complaint? Soviet soldiers allegedly had roughed up Chinese students who led a march against the U.S. Embassy to protest American air strikes against North Vietnam. When Soviet mounted policemen were unable to disperse the crowd of some 2,000 youths, several hundred soldiers broke up the riot. The Chinese Ambassador claimed police brutality and demanded that the Kremlin apologize to the students who participated in the anti-American demonstration. Later the Chinese flew a plane load of students back to Peking and staged an elaborate and well-publicized unloading of stretcher cases and bandaged youths—purportedly victims of Russian brutality. Soon after, Chinese pickets appeared before the Soviet Embassy in Peking.

This farcical episode was the subject of newspaper headlines around the world. Coming as it did on the eve of the subcommittee hearings, it undoubtedly sparked renewed interest in our inquiry. The hearing room was filled to overflowing on most days and many interested persons had to be turned away at the door.

More important, the student incident illustrated how the basic issues in the Sino-Soviet dispute have moved from ideological phraseology to concrete political and martial conflicts. Indeed, this relatively minor yet widely publicized struggle on the snow-covered streets of Moscow indicated the possibility of more significant and more violent clashes between the Soviets and the Chinese.

Few would question, I am sure, that the dispute between these two forces has long since advanced beyond mere polemic. It is now fought on very real political battlefields around the world. From Argentina to the Dominican Republic, and from Tanzania to Algeria, the agents of these great powers vie for the loyalties of those persuaded to the Communist cause. Look deep into the fabric of any underdeveloped nation where Communists are seeking to gain a foothold, and you will find bitter competition between the Chinese and Soviet factions—competition springing from the basic issues in their quarrel.

This brief sketch of the origins and issues of the Sino-Soviet conflict introduces the views of six outstanding specialists on Communist affairs. Although they do not always agree on details of the situation, there emerges from their statement a fundamental consensus on the causes and issues in the conflict.

C. J. Z.

Origins and Issues

1. A Brief History

—ALLEN G. WHITING

The Sino-Soviet dispute is one of the great ideological schisms in history. But, as in other such schisms, ideological differences are as much result as cause. At issue is not merely divergent readings of the "scriptures" of Marxism-Leninism, but conflicts of state interests, a contest over authority and leadership within a presumably monolithic movement, a clash of personalities, and deep differences in nationalist aspirations and feelings.

For years the dispute was held under tight wraps, although points of real difference apparently arose even during the days of maximum collaboration. Signs of discord were discernible in early 1958, but even then special knowledge of Communist jargon was required. For example, Moscow and Peking gave strikingly different public treatment to the desirability and significance of Khrushchev's 1959 U.S. visit and the spirit of Camp David, but this was submerged in endless protestations of continued solidarity.

The first clear manifestation of the depth and seriousness of long-accumulating antagonisms came in April 1960 with the publication by the Chinese Communists of a series of three articles commemorating Lenin. The undisguised theme of these articles was the betrayal of "Leninism" by the unnamed but clearly indicated Soviet leadership. The Soviets responded with publication of what the Chinese Communists described as "hundreds of articles" attacking Chinese views and positions.

Once in the open, the controversy quickly gained momentum: Chinese and Soviet spokesmen clashed within various Communist organizations, and each side began actively to seek supporters against the other in the world Communist movement. The dispute moved from party to government channels as the Soviets applied an economic squeeze on the Chinese culminating in the withdrawal of Soviet technicians from China in August 1960. A special Soviet campaign was launched against Peking's principal supporter, the leadership of the Albanian party.

Soviet efforts to force the Chinese into line at interparty conclaves (first at Bucharest in June 1960, and then in Moscow in November-December 1960) not only failed, but also widened the breach. In the fall of 1961, after further intense infighting, Khrushchev at the Twenty-second Congress of the CPSU openly denounced the Albanian party leadership for "errors" obviously committed by the Chinese. Peking publicly defended Albania with the result that the "Communist camp" became in fact two camps.

The relationship deteriorated further in 1962. From January to April the bitterness of mutual attacks reached a point where both sides appeared to be preparing for an open break. A lull ensued but this was soon ended by the contestants' increasingly damaging moves against each other, and particularly by mounting public evidence that each meant to pursue its own policies without regard to the reaction, interest, or sensibilities of the other. Toward the year's end, clashes over Moscow's handling of the Cuban crisis and the Chinese attack on India demonstrated the degree to which the two antagonists' national interests had been injected into the dispute.

As the focus of the struggle shifted from theory to practice, the arguments became increasingly specific. In 1963 Peking began vilifying Khrushchev by name. He was described as a traitor to communism and as the architect of the restoration of capitalism in the USSR. The Chinese began making it clear that they were demanding the complete repudiation of "Khrushchevite revisionism."

Peking also began revealing historical details in order to buttress its case against Moscow: Soviet "duplicity" in the Sino-Indian border dispute, the Soviet "surprise attack" on the Chinese at Bucharest in June 1960, and the "perfidious and unilateral" abrogation of Sino-Soviet agreements shortly thereafter. The Chinese also accused the Soviets of subversive activities in Sinkiang and warned that China might at some future date seek the return of territories in the Far East and central Asia annexed by czarist Russia.

The summer of 1963 saw the duel move briefly behind the scenes as a Chinese delegation came to Moscow for peace talks. In June a Chinese editorial had demanded Soviet surrender; one month later, while the Moscow talks were taking place, the Soviets published an "open letter" demanding Peking's surrender and blasting the Chinese leaders as warmongers and schismatics. Moscow provoked the Chinese even further by initiating talks with the United States and the United Kingdom on a test ban treaty in Moscow while the Chinese delegation was still there.

Following the signature of the test ban treaty, the Chinese began, in September 1963, the publication of a series of voluminous articles intended as a detailed reply to the July CPSU letter. By the time Khrushchev was ousted a little more than one year later, nine articles had been published. The subjects of the articles provided a good cross section of the issues in the dispute: the greatness of Stalin; the degeneracy of the Yugoslavs; mistaken Soviet views on the national liberation movement; Soviet errors on war and peace and peaceful coexistence; splits in Communist parties resulting from Soviet revisionism, great-power chauvinism and sectarianism; Khrushchev's revisionist views on the peaceful transition to socialism and his renunciation of the dictatorship of the proletariat.

Toward the end of 1963, Moscow suddenly halted its polemic, apparently hoping to persuade the Chinese to do likewise. But the Chinese articles continued: the seventh article (February 3, 1964) called for open struggle against pro-Soviet elements in Communist parties throughout the world, and for the overthrow of Khrushchev.

The Soviet Central Committee met in mid-February to reconsider the Chinese problem. A wide-ranging report by Soviet ideologist Mikhail Suslov (published April 3) hit hard at the Chinese Communists as petty bourgeois chauvinists and Trotskyites and at Mao as the personification of Stalinism. But the crucial issue had become Moscow's effort to organize a world meeting of Communist parties to put Peking in its place. After some temporizing, Moscow in mid-June made clear its intention of pushing ahead to organize a conference, presumably even if the Chinese excluded themselves. The Soviets decided to schedule a preparatory meeting attended by the twenty-six parties that had constituted the drafting commission for the 1960 conference; at the end of July, invitations were sent out for a December 15, 1964, meeting.

The Chinese-oriented parties rejected the invitation, and many other parties exhibited notable reluctance. The box in which Khrushchev found himself (Soviet prestige would suffer either if the meeting were postponed or if it were held with a substantial number of parties absent) may have been at least one of the factors in his ouster. Yet his successors, instead of canceling or postponing indefinitely the December 15 meeting, merely rescheduled it for March 1, 1965.

The Brezhnev-Kosygin team put an immediate end to open anti-Chinese polemics and gave the appearance of trying to normalize relations with Peking. The Chinese leadership responded with a show of interest and dispatched Chou En-lai to Moscow for the November 7 (1964) celebrations. Peking toned down its own polemics, restricting discussion to criticism of "revisionist" policies and avoiding direct attacks on the Brezhnev-Kosygin leadership.

In February 1965, Kosygin visited the Far East to attempt to rebuild Soviet influence in North Vietnam and North Korea and also to seek a basis for some sort of modus vivendi with the Chinese. He made two brief stopovers in Peking and was received once by Mao Tse-tung.

In proceeding with the March 1 conference, the Soviets (in part as a result of pressure from other parties attending) bowed to Chinese sensibilities in important respects: at the last moment, the meeting was described as "consultative" not "preparatory;" and although the final communiqué called for an eventual world conference, the machinery prescribed was so complex that the effect was to put it off indefinitely.

The Soviet leadership, while continuing to hold out an olive branch to Peking so far as ideological polemics were concerned, steadfastly reconfirmed the policies most criticized by Peking. Angry Chinese blasts over Soviet treatment of anti-U.S. demonstrators in Moscow, and equally angry Soviet rebuttals, suggested another period of aggravated relations. The pro-Chinese Albanian party had already strongly attacked the current Soviet leaders by name. Peking later responded to the Moscow meeting with a polemical outburst, promising in effect to try even harder to create and strengthen pro-Chinese parties everywhere.

1965-66 found Peking thrusting hard at Moscow in all international front meetings and in polemical broadsides alleging a "conspiracy with U.S. imperialism" over Vietnam. For its part Moscow stayed out of the public dispute, quietly wooing Peking's erstwhile supporters. By the time of the Twenty-third Congress of the CPSU in March 1966, the Chinese Communists had isolated themselves. In their refusal to attend the Congress they were joined only by Albania, the miniscule Australian and New Zealand Communist Parties, and the wavering Japanese Communist Party which had previously endorsed "unity" in visits to Hanoi and Pyongyang. (Both North Vietnam and North Korea sent delegations to the CPSU Congress.)

Thus Moscow and Peking continued the contest for control over the international Communist movement, varying their tactics only in particulars. The passage of Khrushchev did not abate Chinese Communist challenges against "modern revisionists," and the war in Vietnam did not fuse a new cooperative unity.

2. Common Purpose and Double Strategy

—FRANZ MICHAEL

The Sino-Soviet conflict must be seen not as a clash of interests of traditional nation-states nor as a truly ideological cleavage: it should be viewed as a power struggle between the heads of the two most important Communist parties for the leadership of the entire Communist bloc and movement. The complexity of this power struggle is aggravated for the Communists by the amorphism of their bloc and the Communist movement—by the absence of any structural organization through which the conflict could be resolved.

The dispute finds its main expression in a conflict over priority of strategies through which to advance the Communist world revolution. The contending leaderships place a different emphasis on the use of these strategies, all taken from the common book of Communist warfare. Although the conflict itself is new, the problem of reconciling different Communist strategies is old.

The Soviet Monopoly

Power struggle is inherent in the Communist system. Two factors are involved: First, there is the doctrinal element which asserts that the Communist leadership, through its scientific method, can decide which is the one and only right action for the movement. Secondly, there is the organizational element—the system of democratic centralism. Both elements demand that leadership be in the hands of one man. But there can be no differing opinions on the Communist truth. If there is disagreement in the leading group, the argument must be fought out in so-called ideological terms. The winner will be theoretically right; the loser is the deviationist from ideological truth. This is all the more easily established since the winner of the dispute writes Communist history.

For resolving this so-called ideological fight among the leadership, there is within each party a power structure, a central committee, and a politburo or presidium. Within the parties in power (the bloc parties), disputes are settled by purges. The outsider usually learns of the existence of a conflict only when it is past. Within the non-bloc parties (which exist illegally or legally under the protection of free governments) resolution of conflict is more difficult. However, the controlling group or leader can force the expulsion of an opposing faction, which nevertheless can still continue its opposition. Such is the problem of leadership struggle within each party. The problem of the Sino-Soviet conflict, however, is that of leadership and decision making for the movement as a whole.

Like all Communist leadership conflicts, this conflict is fought in so-called ideological terms. But there is today no central committee or politburo for the movement, and the only organizational structure that exists is the interparty meeting. Moreover, the convening of these meetings and their function have in themselves become a part of the argument. Thus we can follow step by step the spectacle of the ideological accusations and the organizational battle over the question of who has what say in determining Communist policy.

The problem of resolving the power struggle within the bloc and within the movement is in itself new. Lenin's doctrinal concept of the vanguard of the proletariat was international. It implied that there was only one worldwide Communist Party which had its organization or section in each country. And this world party was meant to be organized through the Communist International founded in 1919 by Lenin as the tool of Communist world revolution. The Comintern, which directed among others the Chinese party, was comprised of a congress, an executive committee, and later a presidium (which was regarded as a kind of "politburo" for the movement). But in practice the Comintern was under Soviet leadership, that of Lenin and later of Stalin. The dominant position of the Soviet Party leaders was due not only to the prestige of Lenin and Stalin and the Soviet Party's role in the Bolshevik revolution, but also to that Party's control of the resources of power in one country. The end of this monopoly of power provided the basis for the Chinese challenge to Soviet hegemony.

The Growth of Polycentrism

The dissolution of the Comintern in 1943 did not really change the situation because the control of the movement had already been transferred to the Soviet secret police and foreign service. But the establishment of governments by what became the parties of the Communist bloc provided those parties with their own bases for power and enabled them, if they were far enough from direct control, to defy the attempt of the Soviet leaders to dictate policy. Tito resisted Stalin's attempt to purge him. Chinese leaders in control of the largest Communist party and a territory too remote and too vast to be dominated from Moscow could not only resist Soviet attempts at dominance but, beyond that, could challenge Soviet leadership of the bloc and movement.

The problem had not been foreseen by Lenin. Not only had he tried to establish a world party, but he had also regarded the USSR as the beginning of a Communist world-state controlled by that party. The very name Union of Soviet Socialist Republics was chosen to permit other governments founded by Communist parties to join the union. The short-lived regime established by Bela Kun in Hungary had planned to do so. But when, after World War II, new Communist governments were set up in Eastern Europe and then in Asia, they were of different types and for practical and theoretical reasons could not join. There is evidence, however, that a concept of growing together was maintained not only with regard to what were then the East European satellites but also with regard to Communist China.

The plans of joint development in central Asia and, even more recently, Soviet help in atomic development point in that direction. And though the establishment of new governments and centers of power ended the Soviet monopoly, the prestige of Stalin maintained the Soviet hegemony.

After Stalin's death the situation changed. The actual starting point of the conflict was, according to the Chinese Communists, Khrushchev's de-Stalinization policy of 1956. And indeed, no real conflict existed before that year. The road to success followed by the Chinese Communists and by Mao himself was in full accord with Communist doctrine and strategy as derived from Marx and Lenin and directed by Stalin himself.

Marx had already seen the possibility of utilizing, for Communist purposes, peasant discontent and European nationalist rebellions such as in France, Poland, and Ireland. Lenin, with his theory of imperialism, provided the connecting link of Communist strategy in the West and the East. When the Communist hopes for European proletarian uprisings after World War II were disappointed, the Asian strategy took on primary importance; and China in particular became the test case of the Communist strategy of "anti-imperialism." Since China also became the battleground for leadership conflicts in Moscow, the Chinese story became confused by the anti-Stalinist accounts of the Trotskyite opposition.

The alliance with the Chinese Nationalist Party, the Kuomintang (established in accordance with Lenin's policy in 1923), provided the best opportunity for infiltration and Communist takeover. That it failed was, in my view, not so much due to Stalin's misjudgment or theoretical blunders as to the ability and resourcefulness of the Nationalist leader Chiang Kai-shek who, I believe, almost single-handedly defeated the Communist attempt in China in 1927.

But what has been most misunderstood is the period after 1927. Contrary to most accounts, the strategy that eventually was successful in China—that of rural soviets and peasant guerrilla warfare—was ordered by Moscow itself. Those Chinese Communist leaders who disregarded it were purged—not as scapegoats for a Stalinist policy that failed, as is often thought, but rather as true deviationists. Mao Tse-tung, who came to full power much later than is usually assumed, was no heretic and was not as original as he is today made out to have been. He accepted Stalin's authority even when, after gaining victory in China in 1949, he had to cool his heels in Moscow for more than six weeks before he obtained a less than favorable treaty.

The Role of Mao Tse-tung

After Stalin's death, Mao became a senior leader not only in China but also in the Communist movement as a whole. And the new policy of Stalin's successors further strengthened Mao's prestige. In 1954 Khrushchev and Mikoyan came to Peking to conclude a number of economic agreements which provided the basic Soviet support for the industrial program of China's first five-year plan. This part of the de-Stalinization policy the Chinese had indeed welcomed. But the attack against Stalin and the blame placed on him for a policy of terror in Soviet Russia by Khrushchev at the Twentieth Congress of the CPSU in 1956 greatly embarrassed Mao. It was one thing for Khrushchev to blame his predecessor for the atrocities committed in the past, but it was much more difficult for Mao, who had no predecessor to blame, to switch from the terror of the drives in China to the Hundred Flower Movement (his version of the thaw). He could not very well de-Mao himself. His scapegoat had to be the lower cadres. Mao never accepted the attack against Stalin, and eventually de-Stalinization became one of the sins of which Khrushchev was accused.

But in 1956 Chinese dissatisfaction was overcome by Soviet willingness to help China become a nuclear power. The Chinese participated in the atomic research center at Dubna near Moscow in that year, and in 1957 the Sino-Soviet agreement on weapons development provided the Chinese with a start toward becoming an atomic power. Without that start China would not have a nuclear device today. On that basis the Chinese backed the Soviet Union in their troubles in Eastern Europe, and Mao Tse-tung personally came to the interparty conference in Moscow in 1957 where the Chinese signed the Moscow Declaration with its verdict that war was "no longer a fateful inevitability."

Mao obviously assumed that he would now play a leading part in determining the overall policy for the bloc and movement. At Moscow

University he gave the speech in which he claimed that the "east wind prevails over the west wind" and that the time had come for more aggressive action against imperialism. In Peking, in January 1958, he made a most revealing statement in which he asked for "real," not "formal," consultation on policymaking. But neither was he consulted nor did he receive the additional Soviet aid that he needed. Disappointed, Mao decided to go it alone and initiated his program of the Commune System and the Great Leap Forward which was an attempt to become independent in Chinese economic development, and, with its claim to bypass the Soviet Union on the way to communism, was also a challenge to Soviet leadership. The only remaining basis for this leadership had been the Soviet Union's claim of being the vanguard on the way to communism.

Mao's policy not only ended in disastrous failure but also greatly weakened his position. The challenge to the Soviet vanguard role was taken seriously: it cost the Chinese dearly in Soviet military and economic aid. And in December 1958 Mao resigned from the position of chairman of the Republic, very likely under Soviet pressure. In July 1959, at a central committee meeting, an attempt was made by the leading military member to unseat Mao altogether—a move made, so we are told, with Khrushchev's previous knowledge. It failed and from that time on Mao was Khrushchev's implacable enemy.

Dialogue of Dissent

With the sharpening of the conflict, strategies became the content of argument. In Europe, Communist conquest after World War II had moved up against the industrial West. No guerrilla warfare, no wars of liberation were feasible there. And once the threat of Soviet military might that hung over Europe was checked in the Cuban confrontation, Khrushchev was forced into the all-out strategy of "peaceful coexistence." Proletarian revolution had to take on new clothing. Mao took advantage. Khrushchev became the arch-revisionist who had surrendered to American policy and had been traitor to the cause of revolution; and his very integrity was attacked in a multi-volume research biography.

Much of the so-called ideological argument which followed was a distortion of the other side's stand, quoted out of context and twisted in the best tradition of Communist argumentation. If we compare Soviet and Chinese Communist statements on the basic issues of war and peace they are practically identical. Both have stated that world war is no longer "inevitable," as Lenin formerly had taught, because the "peace camp" had become strong enough to prevent it. Both regard world war caused by the "imperialist mad men" as still possible; both claim that if war occurred "imperialism" would be "doomed" and socialism would win. Both regard "wars of national liberation" as different in character from world war, as "inevitable" and as "just wars." Neither have the Soviets forsworn support of such "wars of national liberation"; nor have the Chinese propagated hydrogen war or excluded a policy of "peaceful coexistence." In fact, they boast to have been the first to assert it in the agreement with India and at the Bandung Conference of 1955.

In answering the Soviet accusations that they were atomic warmongers, the Chinese Communist leaders have claimed that they bore the brunt of battle in the Korean war for the very reason that as a then non-atomic power they could interpose themselves and enter the war without danger of transforming it into an atomic holocaust (between the Soviet Union and the United States) which Soviet intervention might have precipitated.

The Soviets in their turn answered the Chinese Communist accusations that they had transformed the strategy of peaceful coexistence into a policy of surrender to American "imperialism" and into a desertion of the cause of revolution by stating the true meaning of their policy. In a letter of March 30, 1963, to the Central Committee of the Chinese Communist Party the Central Committee of the CPSU stated:

> Peaceful coexistence does not imply conciliation between socialist and bourgeois ideologies.... The peaceful coexistence of states with different social systems presupposes an unremitting ideological, political, and economic struggle of the working people inside the countries of the capitalist system, including armed struggle when they find that necessary, and the steady advance of the national liberation movement among the peoples of the colonial and dependent countries.

Acerbation of the argument between Moscow and Peking has not changed the overall strategic stance of the two contenders for Communist power. The Soviets have been trying to restore unity and have been notably restrained in their answers to Communist Chinese accusations. In their appeal to Peking for unity, they stressed that "what binds us together is much stronger than what divides us." The Chinese have remained deaf to this appeal and have, in fact, refuted it and sharpened the conflict, appealing to their supporters to form their own true "Marxist-Leninist" organizations in opposition to the "Khrushchev revisionists." In their statement of November 11, 1965, published in the *People's Daily* and the *Red Flag,* they claimed that "there are things that divide us and nothing that unites us." And they have gone so far as to declare:

> The antagonism between Marxism-Leninism and Khrushchev revisionism is a class antagonism between the proletariat and the bourgeoisie; it is the antagonism between the socialist and the capitalist roads and between the line of opposing imperialism and that of surrendering to it. It is an irreconcilable antagonism.

If this Chinese policy is carried through, we might see a trend toward the establishment of what would, in fact, be two Cominterns, one led by Peking and another by Moscow—both, however, dedicated to Communist world revolution.

In the course of the argument, the Chinese even challenged the Soviet vanguard position altogether and asserted their own. In October 1963 a Chinese Politburo member, Chou Yang, charged for the first time that because of its revisionist leadership the Soviet Party had lost the claim to be the vanguard of the movement. According to Chou Yang's story, communism had originated in France with the French Revolution; it had moved to Germany with Marx and Engels; to the Soviet Union with Lenin and Stalin; and had then moved farther east where, though it was not mentioned, the leadership was obviously in the hands of Mao Tse-tung. Each of the former leaders had had his revisionist enemies, but each had overcome them. And so the claim for Chinese leadership of the movement was established.

Yet the Soviets have not taken up the glove. In an editorial in *Pravda* on November 29, 1965, they renewed their call for unity, especially in view of the necessity for combined action against

American "imperialism" in the war in Vietnam, expressing their regret that "the effectiveness of joint actions by revolutionary forces was considerably weakened and undermined by differences that arose within the Communist movement." More in sorrow than in anger, they denounced the attempt of "splitting the Communist movement" and decried the effects of the Chinese accusations on the unity of the socialist camp:

> What a gift imperialist propaganda receives from the actions of those who consider it [compatible] with the conscience of a communist to repeat the slanderous fabrications of the ideologists of imperialism about a "capitalist regeneration" of the socialist Soviet state, and who even go so far as to call for an organizational disassociation from the principal forces which are accomplishing the historic mission of building a new socialist and communist society and waging the decisive battle against imperialism.

The Soviets stressed that the effectiveness of Communist assistance to the Vietnamese people depends on the "coordination of efforts of the fraternal parties in socialist countries." They reasserted the Moscow Declaration of 1957 and the Moscow statement of 1960 which, among the various strategies of Communist advance, reaffirmed the resolution to support "wars of national liberation." That "peaceful coexistence" has meant no change in the Soviet attitude toward the strategy of using "national liberation movements" has been reaffirmed in an interview of Soviet Premier Kosygin by an American journalist on December 7, 1965, when, in answer to a question on the relation of a policy of "peaceful coexistence" to the demand for "the right to wage 'wars of national liberation,' " the Premier repeated expressly the Soviet stand: "We believe that wars of national liberation are just wars, and they will continue as long as there is national oppression by imperialist powers."

At the Twenty-third Congress of the CPSU the Soviets have come out even more strongly in support of North Vietnam and of the war of national liberation there. The North Vietnamese representative at the Congress, who received a standing ovation, expressed the gratitude of his party and government for the vast Soviet support in the war. The growing support which the Soviets received among Communist parties for their policies has given them, for the time being at least, the upper hand in the power struggle. They have been more and more conciliatory toward Chinese claims. And even if the Chinese have not given an inch so far, the possibility of a reconciliation may have moved closer—especially should Mao Tse-tung disappear from the scene. The distorted accusations of the two contenders for Communist leadership against each other must not, therefore, blind us to the limitations of the conflict and to the possibility of reconciliation. Even as it is, both the Soviets and the Chinese understand the unity of the two strategies of peaceful coexistence and military action, of proletarian revolution and national liberation movements.

Two Headquarters

Within this double strategy to which Soviet and Chinese Communists both subscribe, "peaceful coexistence" is more deceptive and therefore perhaps in the long run more dangerous. Once understood, it could be handled by us on its terms as the real battle, the battle of the mind, the "ideological warfare" as the Communists would have it. We need not fear that kind of contest if we can shift from a negative, anti-Communist stance to the positive assertion of the principles of our own American revolution and of the multiple values and beliefs of both our Western and the great Asian civilizations. This form of conflict—sparing us the terrible sufferings, sacrifices, and ugliness of any shooting war—is so obviously the one to seek that, unfortunately, we easily forget its dangers—and forget also the Soviet support of the strategy of wars of national liberation.

The Chinese Communists, however, openly propagate the importance and priority of this strategy of national liberation wars. Their leading military man, member of the Party Presidium and Defense Minister, Lin Piao, formulated and reasserted this strategy in its most sweeping form in a statement made September 2, 1965. Repeating Mao's slogan that "political power grows out of the barrel of a gun," Lin Piao reiterated Mao's verdict that "the seizure of power by armed force, the settlement of the issue by war, is the central task and the highest form of revolution." The strategy of guerrilla warfare with its emphasis on the "establishment of rural revolutionary base areas and the encirclement of the cities from the countryside" is the strategy to be followed by "all the oppressed nations and peoples," particularly those of Asia, Africa, and Latin America, in their fight against "imperialism and its lackeys." This strategy is to take precedence over that of proletarian revolution in the industrial countries and is, in true application of Lenin's theory of anti-imperialism, to be used on a worldwide scope. In the words of Lin Piao:

> Taking the entire globe, if North America and Western Europe can be called "the cities of the world," then Asia, Africa, and Latin America constitute "the rural areas of the world." Since World War II, the proletarian revolutionary movement has for various reasons been temporarily held back in the North American and West European capitalist countries [*sic*], while the people's revolutionary movement in Asia, Africa, and Latin America has been growing vigorously. In a sense, the contemporary world revolution also presents a picture of the encirclement of cities by the rural areas. In the final analysis, the whole cause of world revolution hinges on the revolutionary struggle of the Asian, African, and Latin American peoples who make up the overwhelming majority of the world's population. The socialist countries should regard it as their internationalist duty to support the peoples' revolutionary struggles in Asia, Africa, and Latin America.

In the battle for leadership China has chosen to assert itself through wars of national liberation, and it is the strategy of guerrilla warfare that confronts the United States most directly today.

But whatever strategy Moscow and Peking emphasize—we face, in fact, a double-edged threat directed from two communist headquarters. The division—as long as it lasts—may weaken the Communist effort, but it can also lead to confusion and disarray on our side and thus be used to Communist advantage. We must understand the common purpose of all Communist strategies and must counter them in all their aspects.

3. National Interests and the Orthodox Faith

—RICHARD LOWENTHAL

The Sino-Soviet dispute has roots in a peculiar combination of differences between national interests and so-called ideological factors, for the differing internal needs of the two major Communist powers have required increasingly divergent ideological justifications. Thus, in unsuccessfully pressing their national interests upon Moscow, the Chinese have come to attack Soviet policy and to challenge the ideological authority of the Soviet leaders for their lack of revolutionary solidarity.

Unfolding of a Conflict

Rapid growth of Chinese power is not in the Soviet interest, even though China is a Communist state. Yet in her conflict with the United States and her relative isolation from advanced non-Communist countries, China has depended largely on Soviet economic, military, and diplomatic aid. This dependence has led to growing disagreements: on Soviet atomic aid to China; on the degree of Soviet risk-taking on China's behalf (specifically, in wars of national liberation); on the relative value of Soviet diplomatic contacts with the United States (as against total opposition to U.S. imperialism); and on the merits of Soviet aid to independent, non-Communist states like India.

The national situations of the two sovereign Communist countries have been very different. The Soviet Union, for example, puts emphasis on material incentives to assure growing productivity and an increasing standard of living for a climate of internal security; whereas the Chinese, who consider that to retain power at home they require a climate of the besieged fortress, carry on an irreconcilable struggle against internal and external "class enemies." Both the Soviet and Chinese leaders have committed their prestige to rival interpretations of the Marxist-Leninist doctrine.

The Chinese had believed that the political authority of Mao Tse-tung, the leader of their revolution, was more secure than the authority of Khrushchev, the successor of Lenin's successor. Consequently, they believed that Mao's authority was the point of strength from which they could challenge Soviet authority and policy on ideological grounds—for lacking in revolutionary zeal. By so doing, they gravely embittered the dispute because, for an ideological party regime (as Communist regimes are), ideology is the legitimization of its rule. If a Communist leader is accused of not being faithful to the doctrine, it means that his right to rule is disputed. Also, by making the dispute ideological, the Chinese were making compromise much more difficult.

Thus, their separate claims to possess the orthodox faith have led to organized factional rivalry for control of the world's Communist parties and front organizations and have led, in effect, to schism. Because the authority and legitimacy of the leaders is at stake, the dispute has been carried to irrational lengths and has developed a momentum of its own. The Chinese, setting out to get more Soviet aid, lost all. Coordination of foreign policies disappeared completely, even though both powers had major enemies and hence major interests in common. Even the nominal continuation of the Sino-Soviet alliance became doubtful. Territorial claims, which in different circumstances Peking might not have raised for many years, were so dramatized that in the summer of 1964 both sides concentrated troops along the Sinkiang frontier. It was in Sinkiang that the first Chinese nuclear explosion was then in preparation, and the Chinese seemed to fear Soviet military action to forestall their nuclear test. By the time of that test, both sides seemed to be looking for ways to save the alliance.

Post-Khrushchev Policies

There is no evidence whatever, though, that Khrushchev was sacrificed in an attempt to appease China. His successors have been as unwilling as he was to renounce the policy of limited international risks, to surrender their freedom of diplomatic maneuver toward the United States or India, or to abjure the revisionist ideological positions which were developed in the course of de-Stalinization and codified in the 1961 Party program.

The new Soviet leaders hoped that by limited concessions they could revive the alliance, reduce acute tension, and escape from the constant pressure of public ideological attack. If successful, such a policy would clearly be less costly than either surrender or continued all-out ideological conflict.

Khrushchev's successors, therefore, took measures to reduce frontier tension and to resume some material aid to China. They made the first attempt in years to coordinate Communist policies in south-eastern and eastern Asia, particularly in the context of the war in Vietnam. They also unilaterally stopped their offensive ideological polemic, even while continuing to uphold their fundamental position. They virtually abandoned the plan to call a Communist world conference against Chinese opposition, having allowed the preliminary conference of the major pro-Soviet parties to be turned into a purely consultative meeting and to fizzle out in an innocuous appeal for unity and good will.

By now it is clear that the policy of Khrushchev's successors has failed to achieve its major objectives. Although it has reduced the risk of border clashes and saved the formal existence of the Sino-Soviet alliance (important to Red China in case of major war against the

United States), it has not produced coordination of policies or ended injurious polemics. In Vietnam, the Chinese and the Soviets continue to give differing advice to the Communists and to compete for influence, and Peking publicly denounces the Soviet attitude as "soft" and "opportunist." Within the international Communist movement, the Chinese continue their efforts to split pro-Soviet parties and to prepare their own international organization. The Soviet decision not to retaliate and not to insist on a world conference with majority decisions has further weakened Moscow's international authority and influence.

The Proximate Future

What are the chances of resolving the dispute? The Soviet failure to appease China by limited concessions shows the commitment of the Chinese leaders to ideological militancy. Their claim to be the only fountainhead of orthodoxy—even though the Soviet leaders no longer insist on a corresponding rival claim—has become the primary factor in the conflict. It seems unlikely that this Chinese commitment will change so long as Communist China is a poor and overpopulated country confronted with the basic problems of industrialization—problems which might occupy decades. As the first and greatest Communist power, the Soviet Union cannot possibly accept this claim, even from a weak and unstable leadership. It follows that the ideological schism is irreversible under present conditions and will cause a widening divergence of doctrine in the foreseeable future.

Yet this divergence does not necessarily mean increasing hostility between the Soviet and the Chinese Communists. It means only that once the pains of ideological separation are over their relations will no longer be determined by the original ideological bond, but by both permanent and changing factors of national interest—like the relationship between any two great powers. China may be a potential threat to Russia, but as yet she is far from being an actual threat to Soviet security. Nor does Mao consider the present Soviet regime a threat to the security of Communist China. Both are interested in maintaining the framework of their alliance not only as a façade (in order to prove their devotion to unity in competing for influence on other Communist governments and parties) but also as a reinsurance against increased American intervention in Asia. In the future, the more final the ideological split, the more the ups and downs of their formal relations will depend on changing international constellations in the non-Communist world.

In recent years Chinese foreign policy has clearly not been as warlike as Chinese ideological statements. China is interested in maintaining a climate of naked hostility toward the "imperialists" but not in risking all-out war—least of all during the initial stage of her nuclear armament. The chief brake on Chinese aggressiveness has not been Soviet advice but limitations imposed by Chinese military resources. These limitations will persist for a long time in any conflict where the United States is directly engaged, unless Russia is equally engaged on Peking's side. Soviet intervention on behalf of China is unlikely unless U.S. actions seem to be a direct threat to the survival of one or more of the Asian Communist states.

Moreover, the Soviet Union will not soon be forced by Chinese pressure to adopt a Chinese line in its foreign policy or, on the other hand, be driven to an accommodation with the West from fear of China: China is not strong enough to produce either effect. In the short run, the dispute's impact on Soviet foreign policy will show itself mainly as some loss of flexibility, diminishing Soviet capacity for both the creation and the solution of crises, for both aggressive and constructive initiatives. In the long run, the main impact is likely to be a weakening of the ideological element in Soviet foreign policy. The reason is simply that the schism with China is one of the great historical disappointments the Soviet Communists have suffered. It is comparable in importance to the blow inflicted on their faith by de-Stalinization and by the experience of Hungary.

While such a weakening is highly desirable, it will not automatically eliminate existing power conflicts between Russia and the West, particularly the United States. For instance, no ideological motivation is needed for Russia to exploit either U.S. preoccupation with southeast Asia or President de Gaulle's European ambitions for diminishing American influence in Europe.

In Eastern Europe the cohesion of the Soviet bloc under Russian leadership has been greatly weakened by the dispute. This development is unlikely to be reversed. Because of Soviet military and economic power in Eastern Europe, however, it can hardly go much further—short of a major East-West accommodation. Soviet authority in the world Communist movement has been more decisively crippled, so that very little unity of doctrine and strategy remains even within the pro-Soviet wing. This means that the non-ruling Communist parties, big or small, will in the future be much more on their own.

In countries whose internal political and social situations provide no basis for revolutionary crises—in particular, the advanced Western democracies—it will become increasingly difficult for Communist parties to preserve both their distinctive, antidemocratic character and a mass following. Yet, with the support of Moscow or Peking, or both, and with a more independent policy than would have been conceivable in the past, Communist parties may still have opportunities to seize power in developing countries that are suffering from grave economic and social problems and inexperienced regimes. As monolithic world communism recedes into the past, the prospects for communism in the world will depend less on the policies of Moscow and more on the quality of local Communist leadership and the conditions within each country.

Effect on Strategy and Tactics

4. Evolution or Revolution?

—ROBERT A. SCALAPINO

The Communists today are confronted with a great paradox: a pluralism of power and cultural bases, but a continuing monolithism in their ideology. Despite some recent efforts to develop more basic ideological flexibility, the world Communist movement is still forced to operate within the rigid confines of a single "truth."

Ideology, however, is not a primary cause of the Sino-Soviet dispute. Rather, ideology is important because it dictates the form of the argument. The particular vocabulary, the framework within which the debate takes place, the level of intensity of the polemic—all of these factors are strongly related to the special qualities of Marxism-Leninism. Indeed, the rigidities of Marxist ideology contributed much to the intensification of the conflict and to the impossibility of solving it.

The Sino-Soviet struggle, then, relates to the changes that are sometimes described as the movement from monolithism to polycentrism within the world Communist order. The Comintern-Cominform era is over. Now the critical problem for the Communists is how to structure a supranational Communist organization in a period when Communist triumphs have come by means of the nation-state.

A closely related problem for both Chinese and Soviet Communists is their evaluation of internal needs versus external responsibilities. For Sino-Soviet differences have led to purely nationalist conflicts—over border disputes and similar problems. These are secondary and derive from the more basic differences although, in the end, they may be no less important.

An Organizational Stumbling Block

In the basic issue of organization, it is clear that the Chinese Communist Party and certain allies have taken the classical position of the minority—that is, they have placed a heavy emphasis on the equality and independence of each Communist party in any international structure. They have argued repeatedly that within a *single* Communist party the old principles of democratic centralism shall prevail, that the minority shall be controlled by the majority. Among Communist *parties,* however, the principles shall be those of consultation, consensus, and unanimity.

Thus, words like "sovereignty" and "national autonomy" become critical to a movement previously dependent on the theory of proletarian internationalism and the practice of Soviet domination in its international activites. It is obvious today that nationalism has not merely survived communism. In certain respects, nationalism has triumphed over communism and posed, therefore, certain major difficulties. The legacy of Soviet control over the international Communist movement was lengthy and powerful. Soviet leaders, moreover, have not retreated quickly from their heritage of bureaucracy and supremacy. They have made certain concessions to this new era by using words or phrases like "equality" and "no vanguard party." But the full application of equality has been very slow in coming.

Because of the particular nature of the international Communist movement and its ideological base, moreover, the organizational struggle has gradually culminated in a challenge for supreme leadership itself. That challenge has grown from the curious paradox of one truth for many different sociopolitical circumstances. This paradox unavoidably builds into the struggle to determine who is the "correct" leader, the "true" vanguard party. It is similar to the problem within a single Communist Party where ideological monolithism and the very structure of Communist organization have made both the transformation of power and the concept of power-sharing extremely troublesome problems. The tendency, as we well know, has been for a bitter struggle at the time of succession and for a move from collective leadership toward the creation of one-man dominance. Within the international movement, too, it has been exceedingly difficult to permit any real pluralism to exist in the power structure itself.

Communist Family Relations

The second basic issue in the Sino-Soviet conflict stems from the question of how one treats comrades and allies. There is a story, possibly apocryphal, of a discussion between Premier Khrushchev and a Western newspaperman. Khrushchev reportedly said, "Some Communists believe that true communism consists of everyone sitting around a large table, eating out of the same bowl. That is not my idea of communism. It is true that everybody would be very equal, but they would also be very hungry."

This story, true or false, illustrates one fundamental problem of the Soviet Union. It has limited resources, and it must disperse these resources over four great areas. First, it must attempt to maintain military parity with the United States. That is an absolute necessity for retaining its status as a world power. Second, it must meet some of its internal consumer pressures. That too is a necessity if it is to contain internal dissidence and achieve maximum progress at home. Third, if it is really to engage in peaceful coexistence, it must develop an economic aid and technical assistance program for the nonaligned world. Finally, it has certain obligations to its own allies.

The relative degree of emphasis to be placed upon internal demands and external responsibilities has certainly been a critical problem for the current generation of Soviet leaders. It has greatly affected relations not only with China but with other members of the Communist bloc as well. It is precisely within such issues as comradeship and self-concern, generosity and national interest, that many of the specific contentions between Russia and China have emerged. For example, terms and conditions of Soviet aid in the period between 1950 and 1960 caused deep Chinese resentment. In the course of that decade, the Chinese became convinced that Soviet aid was, in effect, blackmail since excruciating economic pressure was applied in an effort to influence Chinese policies. Thus the Chinese could and did accuse the Russians of being old-fashioned imperialists, primarily interested in aid as a mechanism of power.

In addition, the Chinese complained bitterly that their Soviet allies could not distinguish between friend and foe, thus giving aid to the "reactionary bourgeois" Government of India, bolstering that Government's recalcitrance toward China over the boundary issue. They further charged that Soviet "big-nation chauvinism" reached its zenith in the decision to deny China aid in developing her nuclear program. The Soviet excuse was that this would encourage the West to nuclearize West Germany and Japan. The real Soviet intention, argued Mao and his followers, was the hope of maintaining the big-power nuclear club intact—further evidence of an inability to distinguish friend from foe.

The Soviet approach to world problems does place heavy emphasis on the importance of Russian power to the Communist world. The Soviet Union, under this analysis, is both an umbrella protecting world communism and a key to the future revolutionary success of communism everywhere. It is not surprising that the Chinese regard this as yet another sign of Russian "big-nation chauvinism," totally incompatible with revolutionary Marxism-Leninism.

The Way to Victory

Thus, the third important issue in the Sino-Soviet conflict concerns the most promising revolutionary tactics and strategy for the late twentieth century. The Soviet Union would appear to be sincere when it talks about the potential implicit in nation-to-nation competition with the United States. Most Soviet leaders believe that given a few decades they will reach and surpass American productivity. They conceive of peaceful coexistence as a method of total economic, political, and ideological competition. They also support limited military competition, particularly that involving "national liberation movements." On the other hand, they seek to avoid risks that might produce nuclear war. They are convinced that Communist victory can be achieved without global war, providing the Communist world is patient and awaits the growth of Communist (notably Soviet) strength.

The Chinese Communists must think about competition in different terms. They are forced to think about it from a basis of weakness rather than of strength. Their concept of competition therefore hinges much more strongly on the idea of unfolding the world revolution. Unable to undertake sustained nation-to-nation competition with America, they conceive instead of dispersing American power with revolutionary movements promoted at various places around the world. The Soviets can and do accuse the Chinese of following policies that run deep risks of nuclear war, of pursuing an ultra-leftist adventurism that denies the real significance of peaceful coexistence.

This fundamental difference between Russia and China over tactics and strategy bears directly on their differing approaches to the United States and to many related subjects.

A Revolutionary Model

The Chinese will seek to duplicate on an international scale what they so successfully did at home. The Chinese revolutionary model for the world, in sum, is drawn heavily from the model the Chinese developed on the mainland. China now seeks to develop a global united front. It seeks to consider the societies of the Communist bloc as the proletariat. Naturally, the proletariat must lead the world revolution, but first they must be brought under correct leadership. The present false leadership represented by the Soviet Union must be fought to the finish. Only in Maoism does the legacy of true

Marxism-Leninism repose, and only under the type of ideological progression represented by China can the proletariat occupy their rightful place as world leaders.

In Chinese eyes, the Afro-Asian and Latin American peoples constitute the international peasantry, a vitally important class sheerly by numbers and accessibility. Indeed, it is the class that will determine the global balance of power. The peasants must be wooed and won, and the Chinese are placing the heaviest emphasis on this task. But the national bourgeoisie cannot be totally neglected. The Chinese regard societies like France, Japan, and Scandinavia as truly bourgeois states with national interests different from those of the United States. They are perhaps willing to loosen ties with the U.S. and are therefore potential members of a united front. Only the United States and a few of its closest allies remain classified as "big bourgeois" states—compradores who must be isolated and destroyed.*

In another sense, of course, the Soviet Union is categorized with the United States as a primary opponent. Here are two superpowers who threaten to collaborate against China, seeking to exclude her from the nuclear club as in the case of the partial test ban treaty. Hence China must mobilize the rest of the world against these two forces. Both must be classified as imperialist types. Both must be challenged fundamentally—the one for Communist leadership, the other for world influence.

Recently the Chinese have shown much less interest in reaching an accommodation with the Soviet Union or the United States than have the Russians and Americans with them. The present militants of Peking are currently interested in "settlements" only on their terms, and these terms come close to representing unconditional surrender.

Chinese nationalism, currently in a highly volatile stage, is largely responsible for such a reaction. That nationalism begets, among other things, a buoyant optimism—indeed an irrational feeling that the new China can conquer all. The only requirement is to pursue Mao's

---

*Following the preparation of this article, a speech delivered by Lin Piao, Vice Chairman of the Party Central Committee, Vice Premier, and Minister of Defense, in mid-August 1965 dramatically confirmed this analysis of Chinese Communist foreign policy. Marshall Lin used almost precisely the same language as outlined above. For the full transcript, see *Peking Review,* September 3, 1965, pp. 9-30, especially p. 24.

historic command: regard the people as more important than anything else, and unite 90 per cent of them against the remaining 10 per cent—their enemies.

Evolution or Revolution

Soviet strategy, on the other hand, is far more complicated and intricate. First the Russians are struggling hard to retain leadership in the world Communist movement. This requires them to reassert constantly their belief in revolutionary principles. Quite possibly it will also require some revolutionary action if the battle against the Chinese is to be won. At the same time, however, the great Russian advantage over Peking lies in the greater advance of Soviet technology and the more abundant Soviet resource. It is natural therefore that—borrowing from Western policy—the Soviet Union should develop its own program of aid for the "national bourgeois" governments of the emerging world. It is prepared to gamble on evolution even more heavily than on revolution. Its program, moreover, does not hinge upon a simplistic division of the world into Western and non-Western sections: it is so devised as to interact with all parts of the world leadership of Communist-bloc states—aid to "national liberation movements," cultivation of nonaligned states, peaceful coexistence with the "capitalist" world.

The Depth of the Split

As a result of the dispute, probably the deepest problems for the Communists today lie not merely in the erosion of the international authority of the Soviet Union (and possibly Peking as well) but also in the serious factionalism now existing in almost every Communist party in the world. Even if one could assume that some papering over of the Sino-Soviet controversy could take place, the restoration of every single Communist party would be a truly formidable task.

Intraparty disputes in many states are beyond repair. Divisions and rivalries—many of which existed earlier—have often been based exclusively upon personal feuds involving no policy or ideological differences. As a consequence of the split, however, a number of the intraparty squabbles have been frozen, and it will not be easy to reconstruct the shattered parties.

It is conceivable that some cataclysmic upheaval could bring Russia and China into meaningful military alliance. Possibly if China were under direct attack, the Russians would come to her aid, invoking the Sino-Soviet Mutual Defense Treaty. It is even more likely that, for certain limited purposes and periods of time, Russia and China will cooperate or at least pursue common policies in their mutual interests. Any fundamental agreement between the two states, however, would seem unlikely: the radical differences in their internal conditions and world position would preclude it.

Finally, these differences are being interpreted by succeeding generations of revolutionary elites. A first-generation revolutionary elite in almost any society, and particularly in Communist societies, is likely to be strongly ideological and intensely political, to have certain charismatic leadership qualities. A second-generation elite is likely to be more pragmatic than ideological, more technically trained and administratively oriented than its predecessors, and less intensely political. The difference between a Lenin, a Khrushchev, and a Brezhnev is only beginning to be discerned in the evolution of Chinese communism. The problem of personal communication, therefore, between these generations of elites is another factor exacerbating the struggle within the Communist world.

5. A Strange Triangle: China, Soviet Union, United States

—DONALD S. ZAGORIA

If the State Department had consciously set out seven years ago with a Machiavellian plan to separate Russia and China, it could not have played its cards better than it did. Not only did Washington not set out to do this, but its top officials recognized the very existence of the Sino-Soviet conflict only belatedly. Then they were extremely cautious about acknowledging it and, even at this late date, have consciously done little to exacerbate it.

Until quite recently, it was a common belief in Washington that any attempt to "intervene" in the Sino-Soviet dispute might harm our interests by bringing the two Communist powers back together. It will surely be one of history's finest ironies that the power which had the greatest interest in splitting Russia from China was innocent of its own crucial role and deep involvement.

It is, of course, true that at the lower levels of government—both in the State Department and throughout the intelligence community—there were a number of analysts who recognized the earliest symptoms of conflict between Russia and China. But it took a long time before this analysis was taken seriously at the top levels of government.

As late as April 1960, Secretary of State Herter publicly announced that it was too early to tell whether the differences between Moscow and Peking were real or significant. Even as late as 1962, one of the assumptions in the American support of the Geneva settlement on Laos was that the Russians were capable of restraining China in southeast Asia.

Moreover, even among the analysts, myself included, who closely followed the development of the Sino-Soviet dispute from its inception, there was an almost complete lack of awareness of the extent to which American policy has been a cause of the rift. It was the collective failure of Government analysts, officials, and academic specialists to appreciate the enormous impact of our policies on the Communist world.

With the aid of hindsight, a longer time perspective, and some new information released by both Moscow and Peking in the course of their bitter polemic, we are now in a better position to understand our own role in fostering the Communist schism.

The first point to make is that the United States has inescapably been a silent, if largely unwitting, participant in the Sino-Soviet dispute. The Russian-American-Chinese relationship is a triangle in which a change in the relations between any two of the powers unavoidably affects the third. Moscow's imposed relation with Washington has in fact been a key factor leading to the serious deterioration in Moscow's relations with Peking.

Indeed, since 1959, Moscow has been caught between Peking and Washington. If it moved closer to the Peking line on global strategy, it increased tension with the United States. If Moscow moved to ease tension with Washington, it did so only at the cost of increased conflict with Communist China. That is why, when the Russians finally agreed to sign the nuclear test ban agreement, Moscow and Peking came to the brink of a final rupture.

In some respects, the relations among the three powers strongly resemble a lovers' triangle in which Peking plays the part of the aggrieved spouse betrayed by Moscow's "liaison" with Washington. What makes this betrayal all the more unbearable to Peking is not only the fact that the third party is an infidel but, more important, that it is Peking's principal national enemy. It is as though Josephine had been seduced away from Napoleon by Wellington.

Chinese-American Relations

In contrasting the Chinese-American with the Soviet-American relationship, we must first understand that Peking's hostility toward the United States is more deeply rooted than Moscow's. Of the many changing and contradictory elements in Peking's foreign policy since 1957, one has remained constant: namely, that the United States is the main enemy of all "peace-loving" forces throughout the world and that a worldwide united front must be formed against it.

Nearly all other elements in Peking's global strategy are deduced from this basic anti-American line. Peking is too weak to engage the United States directly and, optimally, to remove it from Asia. Hence it sponsors "liberation wars," for example, to weaken the United States indirectly—forcing it to disperse its forces throughout the underdeveloped areas and, ultimately, to bleed itself to death.

Perhaps the main reason for Red China's intense hostility toward the United States is the U.S. support of an alternative Chinese regime a scant 100 miles off the coast of China—a regime which proclaims its intention to reconquer the mainland.

Despite disavowals from the United States that it would support a Nationalist invasion, there are clearly some circumstances in which such support would have to be considered: e.g., an invasion that met with a widespread uprising on the mainland. From the Chinese Communist point of view, this would be the worst of all possible contingencies, placing in jeopardy the very existence of their regime. Even short of that, an alternative regime so close to the mainland could act as a catalyst to dissidence. Moreover, the mainland Chinese fear that U.S. policy is now, or soon will be, committed to a "two-Chinas" solution and that the alternative Chinese regimes on Taiwan will thus gain permanent status. Meanwhile, there is considerable harassment of the mainland from Taiwan, not the least of which comes from overflights by reconnaissance planes.

At the very least, as Communist China sees it, the United States blocks its claim to legitimacy and prevents the culmination of a civil war begun more than three decades ago. At most, the United States and its Nationalist allies hold a dagger at its heart. The situation might be more understandable to Americans if we imagined an American government-in-exile set up in Havana, supported by the

Soviet Union, periodically raiding the Florida coast and proclaiming its intention to conquer the entire country.

There are other reasons for Communist China's intense hostility toward the United States. China has traditionally regarded southeast Asia as part of its sphere of influence, and American power there prevents the expansion of that influence. On China's doorstep the United States props up a faltering anti-Communist government in South Vietnam, intervenes in Laos, and supports a vigorously anti-Communist government in Thailand.

Moreover, India and Japan, China's two principal rivals for leadership in Asia, are also supported by the United States. On the political front, the United States blocks Communist China's recognition by many states and its admission to the United Nations. Although a seat in this body is not one of Peking's highest priorities, it is a symbol of great-power status.

In the economic sphere, it is a result of U.S. policy that an embargo has been placed on strategic materials to China. Perhaps equally important, China is in great need of long-range credits from non-Communist countries, and the United States discourages the granting of such credits.

Meanwhile, in the military sphere, the United States maintains sizable forces in South Korea, Okinawa, and numerous islands in the western Pacific within easy striking distance of the Chinese mainland. While the Soviet Union can announce with some justification that it is difficult to say who is now encircling whom, the same statement cannot and has not been made by the Chinese Communists. There is no doubt in the Pacific as to who is encircling whom.

Add to this the Korean War, in which the United States was a bitterly hated opponent, and the United States represents to China what the interventionist powers of 1918-20, the Nazi German invader, and the U.S. in the cold-war period have been to the Soviet Union.

Russian-American Relations

The relation between the United States and Communist China is quite different from that between the United States and Russia.

U.S.–Soviet relations are still characterized by ideological conflict and the natural hostility of two great superpowers. But the Soviet Union is, much more than China, a satisfied power. It has no irredenta analogous to Taiwan. It is recognized by the world community, the United States included. The Russians have a substantial buffer zone in Eastern Europe under their domination; they are economically more viable than China and therefore less sensitive to economic sanctions. Because of their enormous military power, they feel less threatened by "imperialism."

For all of these reasons, the degree of hostility the Soviets feel toward the United States is mitigated. The conflict of interests between Russia and the United States is therefore not so direct, so complete, and so confining to Russia as is the conflict between China and the United States to China.

Beyond that, the relation between Moscow and Washington is characterized by one fundamental mutual interest: the desire to avoid a thermonuclear war. This tempers Soviet policy.

Peking's Ploy

Viewed in this perspective, one of the keys to the Sino-Soviet conflict and to Communist China's present belligerence must be sought in the state of U.S.–Chinese relations. What the Chinese have unsuccessfully sought to do in recent years is to use Soviet power to weaken the power of their major enemy, the United States.

Peking has, in other words, sought to compensate for its own national weakness by utilizing the strength of its "fraternal" ally to achieve its own national objectives. Because that ally regarded the game as too risky and because its own relationship with the United States required a different policy, it first declined to give Peking the kind of support it wanted. And then it went so far as to make deals with Washington at Peking's expense.

To understand Mao's feeling of betrayal by his erstwhile Soviet ally, one must look back to November 1957 when Mao went to Moscow for a worldwide conference of Communist parties. The conference met at a time when the Chinese leadership's mood might best be described as one of desperate optimism. On the domestic economic front, an agricultural crisis was mounting which soon led to the ill-conceived policies of the "Great Leap." In foreign policy, the Chinese had exuded the "spirit of Bandung" for several years with little success.

One bright ray of hope, however, lay in the Soviet sputnik. The Chinese believed that the sputnik launching and the first Soviet ICBM test which followed meant that the Russians would soon gain military superiority over the United States for the indefinite future. With the balance of power thus irrevocably changed in favor of the Communist camp, the Chinese believed they could at last move quickly forward toward some of their pressing national goals in Asia—particularly the "liberation" of Taiwan and the removal of American power in the western Pacific.

Since Soviet backing against the United States was essential for the realization of Mao's goals, he promptly made a deal with Khrushchev in Moscow. Mao, for his part, threw his weight on the side of the Russians in their struggle with Polish, Italian, and Yugoslav Communist demands for greater party autonomy.

Whereas Mao had only a year earlier backed the Poles against Moscow, he now abruptly reversed gears and called for greater obedience. Khrushchev, for his part, we now know, gave the Chinese a secret military treaty which included a commitment to help China become a nuclear power. At the same time Khrushchev evidently promised greater Soviet assistance in the form of trade, which rose rapidly in both 1958 and 1959.

Probably as a result of this deal, Mao believed that he could count on Soviet support for the first stage of his long-range campaign to eliminate American power from the western Pacific and to assert Chinese hegemony in Asia.

In the late summer of 1958, Mao launched an artillery bombardment against the offshore islands of Quemoy and Matsu. The operation was intended to test the American will and, optimally, to drive a deep wedge between Washington and Taipei. Whatever Mao's precise calculation, however, the operation ended in disappointment—in part because the United States stood firm, but also because, as the Chinese now openly charge, Moscow did not issue a strong deterrent threat to the United States until it had become clear that a Sino-American war was no longer likely and that such a threat could be made without substantial risk.

Khrushchev's Hand

Mao's cause for disillusionment with Khrushchev was, however, only beginning. It was bad enough that in 1958 the Soviet leader would not embark on the forward anti-American policy that Mao expected. But a year later Khrushchev was even engaged in bargaining with the U.S. After sending Mikoyan and Kozlov on scouting trips, Khrushchev himself came to Camp David in October to meet with President Eisenhower. In retrospect it seems clear that this meeting at Camp David was a crucial turning point in Sino-Soviet relations.

Until either Khrushchev or Eisenhower informs us of what actually happened at Camp David, we shall be obliged to speculate about it, for much of their conversation took place with no one present except an interpreter.

Khrushchev's purpose in seeking such a meeting, however, now seems fairly clear. He wanted to translate Soviet strategic power into political gains. In his eyes, moreover, the time was appropriate. The chief American proponent of the hard line toward the USSR, Secretary of State John Foster Dulles, was dead. With Dulles out of the way, the Soviet leader probably thought that he could easily outmaneuver Eisenhower.

The major issue at the time was the critical and potentially explosive problem of West Berlin. The Russians had issued an ultimatum on Berlin a year earlier and the United States had ignored it. It is also likely that Khrushchev was coming to appreciate the dangers of a nuclear confrontation with the United States and that he wanted to reduce some of the risks.

While he was prepared to exploit fully the then U.S. belief in an impending missile gap in the Soviet favor, Khrushchev also realized that he would have to make some concessions to achieve his purposes. As a gesture of good will, he announced a substantial reduction in the Soviet armed forces in January 1960, shortly after returning from Camp David. At Camp David, he had removed the deadline from the Berlin ultimatum. In addition, Khrushchev could offer Eisenhower two major concessions. Both would be worth a great deal to Washington, but would cost Moscow very little.

One of these concerned Taiwan and the offshore islands. Having approached war with China in the Taiwan Straits a year earlier, the American Government was obviously interested in stabilizing the situation there by obtaining Chinese agreement not to use force in the Straits. The United States also wanted Communist China to accept the existence of the Chiang Kai-shek government on Taiwan—a concession Peking bitterly resisted because this would call into question the very legitimacy of the Peking government.

It is not certain that Taiwan and other Far Eastern issues were actually discussed at Camp David, but on the evidence now available it seems likely. The Chinese Communists have charged that when Khrushchev visited Peking on his way home from Camp David, he sought Chinese agreement to a temporary recognition of "two Chinas" and to the removal of the question of Taiwan as an incendiary factor in the international situation. The Chinese Communists must have been furious at Khrushchev's presumptuousness. Not only was the Soviet leader negotiating to ease tensions with the United States—a development in itself disagreeable to the Chinese—but he was also bargaining away the most vital Chinese interest without prior consultation with Peking.

Taiwan was not, moreover, the only Chinese Communist interest which Khrushchev may have come to Camp David prepared to sacrifice. Peking statements assert (and the Russians do not deny) that on the very eve of the Camp David talks the Russians abrogated the secret nuclear assistance treaty they had signed with the Chinese in November 1957. Probably the principal reason for this timing was Khrushchev's realization that if he continued to assist the Chinese in obtaining a nuclear capability, he would greatly limit his ability to control Chinese policy and thus his flexibility in dealing with the United States.

The Final Insult

From Peking's viewpoint, the final act of the Russians' betrayal was their signing of the nuclear test ban agreement in the fall of 1963, an agreement Peking interpreted—and not without some reason—as a device on the part of the nuclear powers to perpetuate their nuclear monopoly. It is still not precisely clear why the Russians suddenly decided to sign a test ban agreement in 1963 after stalling for so long. Sino–Soviet tensions may well have been an important factor.

For years Moscow had been on the horns of a dilemma. It had a common interest with the United States in preventing nuclear proliferation; at the same time, like the United States, it had at least one major ally determined to become a nuclear power. The closer Moscow moved toward a test ban and an agreement on nonproliferation, the more inevitable did a final break with Peking become.

By July 1963 when the Russians after much vacillation finally decided to sign the test ban agreement, it must have seemed to Moscow that conflicts with China had reached such proportions that it was no longer possible or desirable to appease Mao by further hesitation on the test ban. Indeed, the Russians may even have wanted a test ban agreement, which they knew Peking would not sign, as a weapon in their bitter struggle with China for influence in the world Communist movement.

This hypothesis, if correct, would help to answer one of the most perplexing questions about the Sino-Soviet conflict: namely, why Peking—so dependent on Soviet economic and military support—took the initiative in pushing matters to a break. We can now appreciate that Peking felt continued alliance with Moscow intolerable so long as Moscow sacrificed Chinese interests in the course of moving closer to Washington.

The events described above illustrate the crude manner in which Khrushchev attempted to deal with his Chinese "allies" and his apparent lack of comprehension of their national pride. Soviet ineptitude in handling the dispute was, in retrospect, truly remarkable.

There was probably no more heinous insult the Soviet leader could have made to the Chinese than to have spoken on their behalf without first consulting them. Then, having failed to carry them along on a course which he alone had mapped out and which involved consequences undesirable to their position, Khrushchev began to cajole and to blackmail them—notably by withdrawing Soviet technicians in the summer of 1960.

The Chinese themselves, of course, must share the blame for the deterioration of relations. And the United States had no small part as a silent partner in what became a triangular affair.

6. Two Approaches to Military Strategy

—THOMAS W. WOLFE

It is now five years since the Sino-Soviet dispute broke into the open, and at least a decade since it began to simmer beneath the surface of relations between the Soviet Union and Communist China.

Plainly this dispute between Moscow and Peking, who are at once both allies and rivals, is more than a passing quarrel. Even the latest crisis in southeast Asia, though creating new pressures for bloc unity, has thus far failed to bring a real closing of ranks. One might well argue that it is tending to widen the split. Peking continues adamant that the price of unity must be wholesale rejection by the new Soviet leadership of past Soviet policies, particularly Moscow's alleged "collaboration" with the United States. For their part, Brezhnev and Kosygin seem still unprepared to pay a price for unity that amounts to surrender on Peking's terms, although at the same time they may have reconciled themselves to adopting a harsher line in Soviet–United States relations than their predecessor's.

Sino-Soviet Rivalry in the Underdeveloped World

While Moscow and Peking are quarreling over problems of organization and leadership within the Communist bloc, both are also bent on expanding Communist power and influence in the rest of the world. The underdeveloped countries are an important target of this effort. But here, too, the Soviets and Chinese have both supported common objectives and worked at cross purposes.

The essence of the differing Soviet and Chinese approaches appears to be this: The Soviet approach tends to give first priority to the Soviet Union's interests in the power conflict with the advanced countries of the West and only a secondary place to the needs of the national liberation movement in the underdeveloped areas, although it does not deny the importance of the latter.

The Chinese, by contrast, hold that the decisive force in the struggle against imperialism resides not in the industrialized countries but in the national liberation movement in the underdeveloped world. Hence the latter deserves priority when policy claims compete.

In effect, the Chinese formula—borrowing its imagery from Mao's strategy for the Chinese civil war—argues that the prospects are better for revolutionary victory through the "countryside" (that is, the underdeveloped world) than through the "cities" (the advanced industrial countries). In this, the Chinese may have the better part of the argument, for direct Communist advance against West Europe and the United States has not proved notably successful.

Originally there may have been some sort of tacit understanding on a division of labor and spheres of influence between Moscow and Peking, with the latter promoting the anti-imperialist and revolutionary cause in Asian countries and the Soviet Union bearing the load elsewhere. If so, however, the understanding broke down—perhaps around 1955—and has since passed over into sharp rivalry.

There are many differences concerning tactics to be pursued in the underdeveloped world, but the chief one centers on the degree of militancy that is appropriate. Peking argues for a militant and aggressive revolutionary struggle and asserts that such a policy does not entail high risk of military escalation—in brief, that the West—a "paper tiger"—will swallow a large amount of provocation.

The Soviet Union, on the other hand, holds that the revolutionary process can best be advanced under the protective wing of Soviet deterrent military power if unduly provocative local actions are avoided. Though the Soviet Union has not proclaimed itself to be wedded exclusively to a policy of nonviolent revolution, it has displayed a prudent appreciation that ill-timed revolutionary assault may provoke Western intervention and lead to the danger of larger war.

The Nuclear Factor

Behind the Sino-Soviet debate over permissible degrees of revolutionary militance, therefore, lies the dominant question of the risk and potential consequences of war in the nuclear age. This has been a major contention in the Sino-Soviet polemic.

It is sometimes said that the fifteen-year gap between the Soviet Union's initial explosion of an atomic device and China's first such experience helps to account for their differences of outlook on the questions of war and politics in the nuclear age. This is true, but I do not think it is primarily a matter of Chinese ignorance and callousness toward the destructiveness of nuclear weapons, as often charged by the Soviets in their polemic. Rather, I would stress two other points: First, the Chinese have felt there is less risk of escalation to nuclear war than have the Soviets. In effect, Peking has placed a higher estimate on the deterrent value of modern Soviet weaponry than has Moscow itself. Second, not having had their own nuclear weapons, the Chinese naturally have tended to depreciate their significance in comparison with the elements of military power with which China is better endowed. In this connection, it is interesting that the Chinese, while often accusing the Soviets of making a fetish of nuclear weapons, have never hidden their own aim to become a nuclear power at any price. Their nuclear status has enabled them to claim that they have nullified a plot between the Soviet Union and the United States to preserve a nuclear monopoly and "contain" China.

Granted, there is considerable polemical exaggeration in Soviet claims that Peking has irresponsibly courted nuclear war under the mistaken belief that a bright new Communist order could be erected on the radioactive rubble of such a war. At the same time, I think the Soviet leaders have felt a genuine concern about being drawn by Peking into a nuclear confrontation with the West.

On several occasions Khrushchev had even hinted that China, hoping to stand by and pick up the pieces, would like to provoke a war between the Soviet Union and the United States. The Chinese have largely ignored this charge, but they have sometimes urged the Soviets to a bolder course than they themselves seemed prone to take—which might be construed as an incitement along the lines hinted at by Moscow.

Most of the Sino-Soviet dialogue on problems of nuclear war took place, of course, while Khrushchev was at the helm in Moscow. Now he has left the scene. Although there is no reason to suppose that the new Soviet leaders will prove less anxious than Khrushchev to avoid nuclear conflict, their attitude toward the political struggle is as yet unclear. Conceivably they may feel obliged to exploit opportunities for political advance against the West—particularly in the underdeveloped world—more vigorously than did Khrushchev in the latter days of his rule. Khrushchev talked a strong line of support for the national liberation movement, but he was essentially a straddler—neither ceasing to promise Soviet support nor actually tendering it in forms which might risk the unpredictable danger of widening war.

The New Soviet Leadership and Vietnam

The Chinese argue that the United States can be safely opposed and ultimately defeated by waging the political struggle more militantly—at the level of small wars and insurgency actions. Should the new Soviet leaders yield to the argument, they will have made a fundamental decision with far-reaching consequences.

To date there has been mixed evidence on which way Brezhnev and Kosygin may be moving. They have, on the one hand, shown some desire to keep the U.S.-Soviet détente alive; they have avoided major steps that might disturb the delicate balance in Europe; and so on. On the other hand, there have been signs of hardening elsewhere: ostentatious displays of new Soviet weaponry in Moscow; increased organizational activity in Latin America; a sharper propaganda line; and, above all, the new and perhaps critical initiative represented by the Kosygin visit to Hanoi early in 1965 with a Soviet military aid delegation.

The crux of the evolving situation, of course, was the crisis created by the Vietcong attack on Pleiku and the American bombings which followed. The response of the Soviet leadership to the new turn of events was at first guarded. While making loud protests against U.S. actions, as might be expected, the Soviets initially gave encouragement to the idea of some sort of conference to mediate the crisis and bring about suspension of air attacks on North Vietnam. There was also apparently some Soviet tendency to hope that French proposals for negotiation might be forthcoming to get the Soviet Union off the hook. These avenues became less promising, however, as U.S. determination remained firm to persevere until North Vietnam saw the error of its ways while, at the same time, Peking and Hanoi showed little positive interest in the notion of negotiations.

Gradually the Soviet Union moved toward a harder and more uncompromising position. By late February and early March the Soviets took the position that even preliminary talks were out of the question as long as bombing continued. In early April 1965, the Soviet response to President Johnson's April 7 offer of "unconditional discussion" ignored the prospect of discussion entirely; rather, it concentrated on the unacceptability of any settlement which envisaged an independent and guaranteed South Vietnam. Thereafter, the Soviet Union endorsed Pham Van Dong's "Four Points" which, if accepted as a basis of settlement by the governments of South Vietnam and the United States, would amount to outright surrender to the Communists.

To the Soviet leaders in Moscow, it was doubtlessly apparent that their freedom of maneuver was being increasingly narrowed, leaving the prospect of a military solution—to which they would certainly be called upon to contribute—as the principal remaining avenue in southeast Asia. Nevertheless, aware that they would otherwise expose themselves to charges from Peking of "capitulationism" in the face of American pressure and to a further loss of influence among the more revolutionary elements of the international Communist movement, the Soviet leaders seemed prepared to accept a deepening of their commitments in Vietnam. With such developments in the spring of 1965 as the sending of Soviet air defense missiles to the Hanoi area and hints that "volunteers" might be furnished if requested, it appeared that the Soviet Union was moving further along the road toward possible military involvement with the United States in Vietnam. Even so, the Chinese continued to snipe at Soviet policy, charging among other things that the Soviet Union was merely lending sham support to Hanoi.

A certain inconsistency in this criticism was soon evident, for by the end of July Soviet-supplied missile sites had begun to shoot down U.S. aircraft and were in turn subjected to retaliatory attacks. Although this seemed to represent one more step toward a U.S.–Soviet military entanglement, both sides initially avoided open acknowledgment that Soviet military personnel may have been involved, showing common interest in postponing exacerbation of this inflammatory issue as long as possible. In August subsequent repetition of lethal engagements between the Hanoi missile sites and U.S. aircraft likewise found both sides carefully skirting the question of Soviet participation.

Peking's Line on Vietnam

By contrast with the Soviet approach of invoking the danger of nuclear war as a general deterrent and soft-pedaling the question of direct local intervention on a serious scale by Soviet manpower, Peking took a different line, stressing periodically that Chinese manpower stood ready to enter the conflict if need be. As in General Lo Jui-ching's widely noted remarks, they depreciated the prospect that nuclear war might upset the possibility of Communist gains. The Chinese line was particularly evident in early August 1965 when in response to President Johnson's announcement of projected buildup of U.S. forces in Vietnam to 125,000 men, Peking again declared:

"We, the 650 million Chinese people, have repeatedly pledged to the Vietnamese people our all-out support up to and including the sending of our men, as needed, to fight shoulder to shoulder with them to drive out the U.S. aggressors." The object of Peking's threats to introduce outside forces was ostensibly to create the impression that a large land war in southeast Asia might be in the offing, and thereby to induce the United States to slacken its buildup plans and military efforts in the hope of creating a better climate for negotiations.

Thus, as the Vietnamese situation unfolded toward the end of the summer of 1965, Moscow and Peking vied with each other in promises of support, though their declaratory approaches to the situation at the level of military policy showed some distinct differences. In both cases more caution was shown in action than in words. But Moscow, perhaps because of its better capacity to furnish help in the form of modern air defenses, had apparently gone further in its actual commitments than had Peking. Politically, the Soviet position was perhaps more difficult than that of Peking. The latter continued to oppose any concessions for the sake of getting negotiations started, insisting that the United States must give way entirely. Moscow, while taking a somewhat similar *pro forma* stand, probably felt more keenly the need to see the crisis dampened. Therefore its intransigent position was somewhat more awkward to maintain, particularly in the face of Washington's relaxation of some of the conditions it had previously placed upon talks dealing with Vietnam.

For the Soviet leaders, the essential choice seemed to remain what it had been when they embarked on their own policy course toward the Vietnam problem earlier in the year: whether to commit themselves ever more deeply to a dangerous effort to dislodge the United States from southeast Asia, or to seek some way to mediate the situation and avoid the prospect of being drawn into a grave military confrontation with the United States.

In turn, this choice might be said to hinge broadly on the question whether Soviet obligations to the national liberation movement in general and to Hanoi's cause in particular should for the first time be given priority over the Soviet Union's larger national interest. Such interests included: dealing effectively with its accumulated internal problems; improving its competitive position against the advanced countries of the West; and above all, steering clear of the risk of a major war which might ultimately endanger the Soviet Union itself.

Sino-Soviet Military Relations

It is clear that many sources of friction developed in the military area, beginning at least as early as the Korean war. One prime cause of Peking's discontent in the whole dispute was, of course, Soviet withholding of nuclear production assistance, nuclear weapons, and other modern military equipment, after having gone part way in this direction. Whether Soviet second thoughts on helping to build up China as a military power were prompted by long-range foreboding about the future or by more immediate considerations is open to conjecture.

Closely related to the withdrawal of military aid has been the question of the extent of commitment of Soviet deterrent power to the support of China. Ultimately the issue is the validity of the 1950 Sino-Soviet treaty. Soviet assurances have been given frequently, in the course of the polemic, that the Soviet nuclear missile shield extends to China. Indeed, this was part of the Soviet public rationale for withholding weapons. At the same time, the Soviets have left no doubt that there are limits to their commitment and that Soviet military power cannot be counted on—to quote an official statement in 1963—to back "any sort of special aims and interests of China."

Finally, one comes to the question whether the Sino-Soviet dispute may someday bring the military forces of these two Communist powers into collision. This is a prospect which neither side has ever raised in public. Doubt about honoring treaty commitments or fraternal obligations to join efforts militarily has been allowed to enter the picture, but there has been no suggestion whatever that the two might take up arms against each other.

This does not necessarily mean that military planning and deployments by Moscow and Peking are unaffected by this possibility. The concern shown by some Soviet military leaders over reduction of the Soviet ground forces under Khrushchev, for example, may well have reflected their professional judgment that this would diminish Soviet capability for deployments to the Far East without weakening the Soviet posture somewhere else—though no Soviet military man has openly identified China as a problem in this context. Now that China has joined the nuclear powers, it also must be supposed that Soviet military planners are professionally seized with the problem of how this threat might best be met should military conflict with China somehow come about.

Nor does the assumption that a serious Sino–Soviet military conflict is only a remote possibility mean that local border clashes and incidents between Soviet and Chinese military units are to be ruled out. Indeed, reports of border incidents and strengthening of garrisons by both sides along their frontiers in inner Asia during the past year or two suggest that there has already been some harsher friction than is supposed to occur between Communist states. In this connection, it is not without interest that recently released secret Chinese Communist military documents of 1960-61 contained a directive on the need to preserve the security of the Sino-Soviet frontiers of China.

Without question, the deterioration of bonds between Moscow and Peking has gone much further than the shrewdest prophet might have foreseen a decade or so ago. None of this, however, permits one to predict that they are fated to come to blows. While it is not inconceivable that at some future date the two sides may find themselves shooting at each other in earnest, this would not seem likely unless their political relations decline well beyond the present point.

A Matter of Rapport

In closing, it is important to mention the matter of the feelings and attitudes of the Russian people themselves—as distinct from Soviet officialdom—toward China and the Chinese. While we may question how much the people are an effective political force, able to influence directly the policies and decisions of the Soviet leaders, it is nevertheless true in any system that its leaders share to some extent the prejudices and predilections of the people from whom they spring. To put it briefly, the Russian people seem to feel little rapport with the Chinese and seem to regard Chinese ambitions and behavior with considerable misgiving. These attitudes of the Russian people toward the Chinese are perhaps a too often neglected factor in analyses of Sino-Soviet relations.

PART TWO

THE WORLDWIDE IMPACT

Introduction

BECAUSE THE SINO-SOVIET CONFLICT IS ONE OF THE GREAT SCHISMS OF HISTORY, its shock waves have been felt in Warsaw and Bucharest, in Hanoi and Djakarta, in Havana and Dar-es-Salaam. It has contributed to the growth of polycentric tendencies in Communist parties both in and out of power. The conflict also has had its effects on the leaders of non-Communist nations. It has added a new set of variables to the process of making foreign policy, thereby further complicating an already agonizingly complex global scene.

In Part II the effects of the rift are traced in Eastern and Western Europe, Asia, Latin America, and Africa. Communism has scored its greatest successes in Europe and Asia: besides the Soviet Union and China, there are three Communist regimes in Asia and eight in Europe. Some of the non-Communist countries in Europe and Asia have important Communist parties: Indonesia, India, Italy, and France immediately come to mind. These and other nations are analyzed in Part II by ten specialists to determine how and to what extent the effects of the Sino-Soviet conflict have been felt, both inside and outside the Communist bloc.

The profound impact of the Sino-Soviet conflict was brought home to me in June 1965 when I visited Eastern Europe as the President's representative to the Poznan, Poland, Trade Fair. The occasion provided the opportunity to tour both Poland and Czechoslovakia and to speak to government officials and private citizens in both countries.

In Czechoslovakia, the Sino-Soviet split appears to have hastened the process of "thaw" which began about two years ago. Although changes in the Czech system were occasioned by the country's economic stagnation, the Sino-Soviet conflict allowed the regime in Prague more room to maneuver in ending the downward slide of the economy. Today travel between Czechoslovakia and the rest of Europe is fairly free. Czech writers and artists are experimenting with new forms. There is public discussion of economic and social problems. Economic reforms are more "revisionist" in some aspects than those accomplished in Yugoslavia. Contacts with the West are expanding rapidly. A feeling of change is in the air.

This does not mean, of course, that any basic change has taken place in the Communist system of government in Czechoslovakia. The leaders have not changed and their ties to Moscow are close. The Czechs are still under the domination of communism, but communism which is adapting to reality and, in a sense, becoming rather "humanized." Czech officials, for example, parroted the Kremlin line about U.S. efforts in Vietnam, but they did so with marked restraint.

This restraint was in stark contrast to the attitude of the Polish government and controlled Polish press which have stridently condemned American bombing in North Vietnam. In my talks with Polish officials, I found them both vehement and vociferous on the Vietnam issue. It seems to me that this attitude springs from a sense of frustration. For several years the Poles have tried to mediate among factions in the Communist world, especially between the Soviet Union and Red China. As Sino-Soviet differences over Vietnam have grown sharper, Polish authorities have become anxious and nervous. They apparently fear that Poland may—through the Soviet Union—be drawn into a war in southeast Asia, or that a complete Sino-Soviet break ultimately may result in a return to rigid Kremlin control of the satellites as during the Stalin era.

I would like to stress that I saw no evidence that the people of Poland share their government's views on U.S. activities in Vietnam. Most of those to whom I spoke could not be less concerned about what happens in southeast Asia. They are interested, however, in the Sino-Soviet conflict. Peking's open defiance of Moscow's wishes gratifies their own deep antipathies toward the Soviet Union. Although they cannot protest against Kremlin domination, they can take vicarious pleasure from Chinese polemics.

Even in Poland, however, there are some who are willing to speak out despite the high risk of punishment. An example is an incident which occurred during my stay in Cracow. Although the Polish press virtually ignored my visit, a group of Cracow youths learned from Radio Free Europe broadcasts that I would be in their city. They searched the city until they found our American cars outside the hotel. When our party came out, one of the young men approached me and placed in my lapel a pin with the initials "PW" in the form of an anchor. This emblem had been the mark of the Polish resistance against Nazi occupation during World War II. The initials stand for "Polska Walczaca," which means "Fighting Poland." The young men explained that today it is the symbol of those who are fighting for freedom—this time against Communist domination. To them, communism, whether of the Peking or the Moscow variety, is a shackle on the spirit of man.

C. J. Z.

Europe

1. The Communist States of East Europe

—MARIAN A. CZARNECKI

The Sino-Soviet dispute erupted during a period of mounting tensions within the Communist world, accelerating the tempo of change in Central and Eastern Europe and reinforcing certain trends which found their first expression in Yugoslavia's defection in 1948 and in the post-1956 developments in Poland. By undoing the ideological unity of the Communist movement, the conflict between Moscow and Peking served to intensify factionalism within the Communist camp and to change its character. It also afforded the regimes of Central and Eastern Europe unique opportunity to assert a measure of independence from the Soviet Union. Most of them took advantage of the opportunity to embark upon their separate "national roads to socialism." The resulting tendency toward polycentrism, anticipated by Togliatti (leader of the Italian Communist Party), fragmented the once monolithic Soviet bloc and reduced Soviet control over Eastern Europe.

Overhauling the Communist Bloc

Apart from Tito's defection, the unity of the Soviet bloc continued unbroken until 1956. Ideological conformity, widespread application of Stalinist policies, and overbearing military power reinforced Soviet hegemony over Central and Eastern Europe. In Stalin's view, the Communist regimes of Eastern Europe were first and foremost the agents of Moscow. They were expected to, and did, conduct themselves as behooved the Soviet Union's satellites, obediently carrying out Moscow-dictated policies with little regard for the nature and the traditions of their own countries.

Three developments converged in 1956 to alter that situation. Khrushchev, attempting to reach the pinnacle of power in the Soviet Union, made his formal break with the Stalinist past at the Twentieth Congress of the CPSU. During the same year, popular discontent in Eastern Europe found its most dramatic expression in Poland's "spring in October" and in the Hungarian revolution. Forced to choose between the employment of physical power to maintain the status quo and the fashioning of a viable system through the establishment of a new pattern of relations with the Communist camp, Khrushchev chose the latter. In the course of the subsequent reconstruction of the bloc, the satellites were granted a considerable degree of autonomy in domestic affairs at the price of strict subordination to Soviet foreign policy and ideological authority. Although he obviously desired that every Eastern European country continue to conform roughly to the Soviet model of Marxism-Leninism, Khrushchev believed that diversity was not incompatible with harmony. He accepted the possibility that socialist development would take different forms in different countries. At the same time, he did not encourage any regime to hold up its deviations as a legitimate example for others to follow. He also began to search for new means which would, on the one hand, strengthen the ties of self-interest binding each member state to the bloc and, on the other hand, make possible more effective Soviet control over the entire area.

The reconstruction of the bloc produced the greatest changes in Poland. Making use of his newly gained authority, Gomulka insisted upon and secured the removal of the key supervisory Soviet personnel in Poland. He also terminated the campaign of forced collectivization of agriculture; did away with many of the outward expressions of the repressive rule put into effect during the Stalinist period; reached a modus vivendi with the Catholic Church; allowed the people—including artists, writers and other exponents of the cultural life of Poland—a modicum of free expression; and began to experiment with economic reforms.

In spite of the introduction of these substantial changes, Gomulka's deviationism operated within clearly defined limits: he acknowledged Moscow's ideological supremacy and adhered closely to Khrushchev's line in international affairs. In time, his loyalty to Khrushchev and his success in maintaining effective Communist rule in Poland without resort to overt repression won him a solid reputation among the leadership of the Soviet camp. It is a measure of his prestige that, in the fall of 1965, he alone among the East European Communist leaders received a visit from Brezhnev and Kosygin who apparently traveled to Poland to explain to Gomulka the reasons for Khrushchev's removal from office.

Until the public manifestation of the Sino-Soviet rift, no other regime of Central or Eastern Europe—except Yugoslavia—had atttemped innovation on the scale of Gomulka's experiment in Poland. To most Communist leaders, internal liberalization was frought with grave dangers: Once they began to tolerate public dissent, or acknowledged by policy changes the effectiveness of popular pressure as an instrument of reform, where would the process end? Who could guarantee that rights restored to the people, even on a very modest scale, would not produce demands for greater concessions? What would this do to the job security of the current Communist leaders? In addition, Khrushchev was neither immortal nor omnipotent: what if his successors decided to turn back the clock? Clearly, to most of the Communist leaders of Eastern Europe the abandonment of the Stalinist heritage involved too large a risk. During the next four years nothing dramatic happened in Eastern Europe. Under the surface, however, a tug of war began between the exponents of revisionism and the entrenched defenders of the old order.

A Choice of Ideology

By 1961, the ideological fabric of the Communist world was beginning to show internal strain. The controversy between Moscow and Peking was evident at the Twenty-second Congress of the CPSU in Khrushchev's bitter denunciation of Albania's General Hoxha and in the quiet removal of the "anti-party group" consisting of Molotov, Malenkov, and Kaganovich. The conflict was now in the open. Peking's increasingly strident challenge to Moscow as the fountainhead of orthodoxy in Communist ideology began to reverberate throughout the Communist world. The Communist elites of Eastern Europe—and of other geographical areas—found themselves confronted with not one but two sources of ideological authority—each propounding a different interpretation of Marxism-Leninism, each contending for adherents to its own interpretation.

For the first time, these elites could make a choice: They could align themselves with one of the two great powers of the Communist world. They could attempt to straddle the fence or seek to advance their own interests by playing Moscow against Peking. Formerly the entire Communist movement was subordinated to the security and power interests of the Soviet Union; now each national party elite began to assess its own interests independently and to act accordingly.

Similarly, the various factions within the national Communist establishments were no longer restrained in the pursuit of their respective ambitions by the necessity to adhere to a single interpretation of Marxism-Leninism. With the appearance of the second center of Communist ideological orthodoxy, both the pattern of the factional conflicts and their resolution changed. The different factions could now choose from alternative ideological justifications to explain and support their programs. Once the breach was made, deviations from established policies and rationalization of economically—or politically—expedient decisions became less risky even for minority or fringe factions.

Nevertheless, the opportunities for ideological innovation and revision presented to the Communist leaders of Central and Eastern Europe by the Sino-Soviet split were not unlimited. The proximity of Soviet troops and the example of Khrushchev's violent reaction to Hoxha's deviation argued against any rash decision to take up Mao's cause. The experience of the Hungarian revolution also demonstrated that the regimes of Eastern Europe continued to occupy their privileged positions by virtue of Moscow's active support. Soviet troops, rather than their own national security forces, remained the ultimate guarantor of their security.

Moreover, the innovations in Communist ideology and practice emanating from Moscow were basically more congenial to the East European Communist leaders than the hard line pursued relentlessly by the Chinese. "Peaceful coexistence," the reestablishment of economic and cultural contacts with the West, and the conditional right to pursue their national roads to socialism held more appeal to these men than the aggressive form of world revolution preached by Peking. As rulers of small and generally impoverished countries, the East European regimes evidenced little enthusiasm for supporting "wars of national liberation" all over the globe. The conflict in Korea had resulted in an unwelcome imposition on their meager national economic resources. The prospects of a continuing drain of their limited resources to hasten the goal of Communist world revolution held even less appeal.

Prompted by these and related considerations, most of the Central and East European Communist regimes eventually sided with Moscow on the basic ideological issue of the Sino-Soviet dispute. However, since the occasion presented them with an opportunity to assert themselves, they chose to determine individually how and when they would give expression to their decision. Consequently, the timing and form of their commitment to Moscow and their public disagreement with Peking differed from country to country.

Albania: A Separate Course

The one exception was provided by tiny Albania which, with a population of approximately 1.3 million, occupies an area comparable to that of the State of Maryland. A mountainous country with resources inadequate to provide its population a reasonable standard of living, Albania never enjoyed a stable position either within the Communist world or vis-à-vis its neighbors. At various times, Yugoslavia, Italy, and the Soviet Union have sought to control its government. Partly because of this experience and partly because of the ideological and political inclinations of its leaders, Albania chose to chart its own course in Eastern Europe.

The ideological outlook of the Hoxha and Shehu regime derives from the fact that the process of de-Stalinization taking place in Eastern Europe during recent years has made no impact on life in Albania. As a matter of fact, Khrushchev's actions at the Twentieth and Twenty-second Congresses of the CPSU, and his encouragement of partial internal liberalization, left the Albanian regime increasingly restive. The final straw came when the Soviet leader made friendly overtures to "revisionist" Tito, whom some Albanians consider the prime threat to their continued national existence. There are nearly one million Albanians living in Yugoslavia, and the prospect of an attempt to reunify all Albanians under Yugoslav auspices undoubtedly caused Hoxha and Shehu many sleepless nights. In any event, as soon as the opportunity presented itself in the form of the widening Sino-Soviet breach, Albania bolted Moscow's protectorate and aligned herself squarely with the Communist Chinese. In return for becoming Peking's bridgehead in Europe, she obtained Chinese Communist political support and modest economic assistance. The latter has been barely sufficient to enable Albania to maintain even its present low standard of living.

East Germany and Bulgaria: Loyal Followers

Of the bloc members who took Moscow's side in the confrontation with Peking, Bulgaria and East Germany warrant brief comment. The Zhivkov and the Ulbricht regimes are heavily dependent on Moscow. When confronted with a choice, both responded in a predictable manner: they immediately declared complete loyalty to Khrushchev and engaged in a public polemic with Mao. Since that initial commitment, neither regime has attempted to modify its position or to exact any concessions from Moscow for its support.

The nature and the extent of Soviet involvement in East Germany made Ulbricht's action in this instance inevitable. He undoubtedly would have preferred to side with Mao. The tyrannical character of his rule and his pre-1961 public expressions of admiration for the Red Chinese support this conclusion. Nevertheless, Ulbricht could not ignore the fact that he has been kept in office by the Soviet divisions stationed in East Germany and that he could be replaced without notice. This utter dependence on Moscow made him swallow insults on previous occasions. As one expert on Communist affairs wrote recently, Ulbricht "must always remind himself of the painful truth that he will always be a satellite whom Moscow can afford to ignore."

Zhivkov's reasons for espousing the Soviet position were equally compelling. Direct Soviet involvement in the internal affairs of Bulgaria was more pervasive than in any other area of Eastern Europe, except East Germany. Economically, Bulgaria's dependence on the Soviet Union continued to increase in proportion to the current regime's growing record of economic failure. In 1964 alone, Soviet loans to that country amounted to more than 500 million rubles. Politically, the visit to Sofia of Soviet party leader and theorist Suslov following the abortive coup suggested that the Soviet Union was keeping a very close watch on the internal developments in Bulgaria. It had been reported that Zhivkov was alerted about the incipient coup not by his own internal security forces but by Soviet agents. If that is the case, Bulgaria's Premier and Party First Secretary had good reason to stay on the best of terms with the powers in Moscow: his security depended on it.

Poland, Czechoslovakia, and Hungary: Advancing National Interests

The Communist leaders of Poland, Czechoslovakia, and Hungary followed different paths while siding with Khrushchev on the basic issue of the Sino-Soviet split. In the process, each made some advances along his separate road to "national socialism."

In Poland, by 1961, the blossoms produced by the "spring in October" were fading rapidly. Having achieved a modicum of de-Stalinization which made Poland, during the preceding four years, the most progressive member of the Soviet bloc, the Gomulka government appeared to have reached the limit of its ambition to innovate. The Chinese challenge to Moscow did not serve to revive the drive for change and internal liberalization in that country. In two other respects, however, the controversy left its mark on Gomulka's attitude and policies: his persistent efforts to mediate the dispute and to dissuade Khrushchev from a collision course with Red China gave him added stature among the leaders in the Soviet camp; he leaned on this asset to advance Poland's national economic interests even when these began to clash with Khrushchev's designs for reestablishing Soviet hegemony over Eastern Europe through the Council for Economic Mutual Assistance (COMECON).

Czechoslovakia's Antonin Novotny took a different route. He was obviously loath to part with Stalinist ways. At the same time, he realized that Khrushchev needed his support in the confrontation with Red China and would be less apt to interfere in Czechoslovak affairs if he received it. Novotny's response was prompt and practical. He gave Khrushchev his complete loyalty in the struggle with the Communist Chinese while simultaneously taking action against domestic reformers who, using the proceedings of the Twenty-second Congress of the CPSU as a springboard, attempted to promote internal liberalization in Czechoslovakia. (Vice President and Politburo member Rudolf Barak, a leader of the reform movement, found himself in jail for theft in spite of his reported personal friendship with Khrushchev.) The process of de-Stalinization has been taking root in Czechoslovakia while domestic economic reforms, currently under discussion, promise to alter drastically the structure of the Czechoslovak economy.

For Hungary's Kadar, the call to make his choice presented certain problems. He owed a debt of gratitude to Khrushchev, who had installed him in power and who had shown continuing concern about maintaining the political stability of the regime. Until the emergence of the Sino-Soviet rift, Kadar was repaying that debt by faithfully following Khrushchev's directives. To continue on this course would entail not only taking issue with Red China but also embracing Khrushchev's program of liberalization. This alternative was not without some dangers. The Hungarian people were restive; party *apparatchiks,* firmly entrenched in positions of authority throughout the country, viewed internal liberalization as a direct threat to their power. The question which confronted Kadar was: could he follow Khrushchev down the line while retaining control over the regime and the country?

Whatever doubts Kadar may have entertained about the practical wisdom of his decision, he gave Khrushchev his full support and, slowly at first, embraced a program of internal liberalization. Under the standard of "national reconciliation," he attempted to heal the wounds of 1956 and to harness the energies of the Hungarian people to the task of national socialist construction. Although his success with respect to the latter has been rather limited thus far, his advocacy of Hungarian nationalism appears to have earned him some stature in his own country and has partially replaced the image of a puppet installed by the man who had crushed Hungary's revolution.

Rumania: Exploiting the Split

Of all the countries of Central and Eastern Europe, Rumania appears to have attempted and gained the most from the ideological schism. In four years, through skillful and relentless exploitation of the Sino-Soviet conflict, Gheorghiu-Dej managed to assert a larger measure of independence from Msocow than that enjoyed by any other East European country save Yugoslavia. It is worthy of note that the process of "de-satellization" of Rumania came first and was only later followed by some measure of domestic liberalization in the political and cultural fields.

Gheorghiu-Dej, whose march along his separate road of socialist construction began with his differences with Khrushchev over Rumania's economic policy, refused to sacrifice his own plans for heavy industrialization of Rumania to Khrushchev's attempts to promote economic —and then political—integration of Eastern Europe through the device of the "socialist division of labor" within the bloc. Gheorghiu-

Dej was largely instrumental in blocking Khrushchev's plans to establish certain supranational (and Soviet-controlled) agencies within COMECON. Having achieved this, the Rumanian leader proceeded to implement his own national economic plan. His rupture with Khrushchev was subsequently formalized in a declaration of the Central Committee of the Rumanian Communist Party. It opposed any attempt to elevate supranational planning to the level of an ideological principle. This remarkable declaration also rejected all forms of economic cooperation among the Communist states that would involve an infringement of national sovereignty; forcefully reasserted the independence of all Communist parties; and warned against attempts on the part of any national party to interfere in the affairs of another.

This public display of insubordination must have been galling to Khrushchev and, were it not for his difficulties with Mao, he could have been expected to act swiftly to force the Rumanian Communist leadership back into line. The Chinese Communists, however, have long insisted on the economic sovereignty of every "socialist" state and gave Dej their full support on this issue. Further, Khrushchev was in the process of wooing Yugoslavia; an attempt to bring physical pressure to bear on Gheorghiu-Dej for following Tito's example could have proved embarassing. Khrushchev apparently decided not to risk any further dissension within the Soviet camp, and Gheorghiu-Dej went unpunished.

Rumania's assertion of independence from Moscow was not confined to the area of economic policy. In 1963, Rumania became the first—and thus far the only—country in the Soviet camp to review diplomatic relations at the ambassadorial level with Albania. During that same year, Gheorghiu-Dej refused Khrushchev's invitation to attend a meeting of the East European Communist leaders in East Germany. In the United Nations, Rumania voted with Yugoslavia in support of a resolution calling for an atom-free zone in Latin America. (The rest of the Central and East European countries followed the Soviet Union's example and abstained from voting on that proposal.) In 1965 Rumania again broke the line by refusing to send a delegation to Moscow for the consultative meeting which witnessed the demise of Khrushchev's plans for a direct confrontation with the Chinese

Communists within the framework of a world conference of Communist parties.

Although Gheorghiu-Dej has died, Rumania is continuing on its independent course, endeavoring to strengthen relations with Yugoslavia and to establish increased economic contacts with the West. Relations with the new Soviet leadership appear friendly if somewhat distant. Bucharest has not been above flirting with Peking when this appeared to serve its purpose. At the same time, Rumania has not attempted to withdraw from any of the basic intra-bloc arrangements—such as the Warsaw Pact and COMECON. Instead, it abides by those commitments but only to the extent that they do not interfere with the advancement of Rumania's national interests.

Yugoslavia: A Mutual Accommodation

Whereas the Sino-Soviet dispute has tended to weaken the bonds which united Moscow with most of Eastern Europe, it had the opposite effect on Soviet-Yugoslav relations. Khrushchev, anxious to achieve some semblance of harmony in Eastern Europe and thereby to solidify his own position in the struggle with Peking, made an active effort toward reconciliation with Tito. He was willing to suffer Yugoslavia's independent course in foreign affairs in return for an accommodation on intrabloc matters. Specifically, he wanted Tito to join the Soviet-led camp in the controversy with Peking and to stop flaunting Yugoslav revisionism and urging other East European countries to follow his example. From Tito's standpoint, Khrushchev's overtures could not have been more timely. Plagued by economic problems at home, by growing dissension between the constituent republics of the federation, and by increasingly sharp factionalism within his own party, Tito was in a mood to welcome an improvement of his relations with Moscow and with Eastern Europe generally. The reconciliation was effected in 1962 and during the past four years Yugoslavia, while retaining its independent foreign policy, has become more closely associated with the Soviet camp. During 1964, Tito visited—or was visited by—all of the Communist leaders of Eastern Europe and secured for Yugoslavia associate status within COMECON. It remains to be seen how future developments in Sino-Soviet relations will affect this new direction in Yugoslavia's policy toward her neighbors in Eastern Europe.

In retrospect, the conclusion appears inescapable that the schism which rent the ideological unity of the Communist world played a substantial part in stimulating the process of change in Central and Eastern Europe. Admittedly, earlier factors had already prepared the ground for these developments and provided the initial impetus. These included the examples of Yugoslavia and Poland, Khrushchev's innovations, United States foreign policy, and the resurgence of nationalism in that part of the world. Nevertheless, the climate created by Mao's successful challenge of Soviet ideological supremacy loosened one of the vital bonds which had united the Communist world. It provided an invitation to deviationism and contributed to the erosion of Soviet dominance in the satellite countries: Eastern Europe is very different today from what it was just five years ago.

2. West European Communist Parties: France and Italy

—ALVIN J. COTTRELL
—ANNE M. JONAS

The Sino-Soviet dispute has had an impact on all the Communist parties of Western Europe. This impact has varied from country to country since "West European communism," in a generic sense, does not exist. Each party must be analyzed separately if its interactions with Moscow and Peking are to be understood in depth. Nevertheless, two generalizations may safely be made.

First, many of the Communist parties of Western Europe have gained increased maneuverability as a result of the Sino-Soviet dispute. Moscow's role as the "bastion of the revolution" has been further challenged by the dispute; developments in Soviet policy since Stalin's death have enabled some Western European parties to gain a more independent position vis-à-vis Moscow than it was possible to attain under the earlier, more monolithic arrangements. Hence, although the majority factions in all of the West European Communist parties still tend to side with Moscow rather than with Peking on all essential issues under debate, many of these parties are questioning the extent to which their own domestic policies and programs should be dictated by the USSR.

Second, the lesser parties of Western Europe have been more vitally affected by the conflict than have the larger ones, primarily because their organizational structures render them more susceptible to criticism from aggressive minority factions. In Belgium, for example, a pro-Chinese splinter group has emerged which has been bold enough to preempt the name of the older, pro-Soviet party and to present itself as the true representative of bona fide Communism. But the fragmentation of the Communist Party in Belgium—and lesser fragmentations of the party in some of the other smaller nations of Western Europe—has remained primarily an intraparty problem. Within their respective countries, the smaller Communist parties are, for all practical purposes, dissident minority groups exerting marginal influence on national policy.[1] Whatever the groupings and regroupings of their respective factions, their responses to the Sino-Soviet dispute constitute, in essence, little more than another page in the history of that internal dissension which has plagued all Communist parties everywhere since the beginning of the international Communist movement.

By contrast, in both France and Italy, since the end of World War II the Communist parties have had a major influence on domestic politics. Both the French and the Italian Parties have demonstrated a capability throughout most of the postwar years to command the support of at least 20 to 25 per cent of the electorate in all important contests at the polls. The French and the Italian Parties are, therefore, the two most important Communist Parties in Western Europe today. This analysis will concentrate on a comparison of the reactions of these two parties to the Sino-Soviet controversy.

The French Communist Party

As 1965 drew to a close, the Sino-Soviet dispute had affected the Communist Party of France (PCF) in three ways: First, it had necessiated that Maurice Thorez, head of the Party for thirty-four

[1]The authors exclude here the Finnish Party, which they do not consider to be a Western European Communist party.

years prior to his death more than a year ago, reconcile his continued use of a rigid, monolithic party machine—tightly controlled from the top and long identified with Stalinism—with the "liberalization" trends emanating from Moscow. Second, the Sino-Soviet dispute had given rise, along with other factors, of several purges and withdrawals from the Party of key second-echelon leaders. Third, it had exacerbated serious differences between the Party and one of its principal youth organizations over preferred programs and methods of control.

Prior to the advent of Maurice Thorez as leader of the PCF about 1930, the French Communist Party was deeply divided and faction-ridden—a comparatively ineffective movement. Thereafter, Thorez gradually built up a tightly controlled, highly disciplined organization along the Stalinist model. Under his leadership, the PCF became an increasingly effective influence on French domestic politics. Khrushchev's "secret" speech to the Twentieth Congress of the CPSU denouncing Stalin's methods and his "cult of personality" proved particularly embarrassing for Thorez. He immediately asserted that problems associated with the "cult of personality" did not apply to the PCF and sought to tone down Khrushchev's denunciations of Stalin for the consumption of his own party faithful. Stalin, the official organs of the PCF argued, had been guilty of "errors"; but these "errors" never were presented by the PCF as the bloody crimes Khrushchev had accused Stalin of having committed. Khrushchev's "secret" speech never was published or circulated by the PCF; when it became available in France through other sources it was persistently referred to by the PCF as a pronouncement *alleged* to have been delivered by the Soviet leader.

Despite his apparent initial underestimation of the impact of de-Stalinization on the PCF, Thorez soon had to cope with those disturbances within the party elite and within the rank and file which were the inevitable aftermath first of de-Stalinization and later of deteriorating relations between the USSR and Communist China (the CPR).

The ensuing dissension within the PCF also was rooted in the objections of some key party members to Thorez's rigid approach to domestic issues confronting the party. Increasingly, with the rise in living standards of the working class under a capitalist economy that was rapidly recovering from the ravages of World War II, the identification of the French "proletariat" with the PCF was diminishing. Certain leaders of the French trade union movement—including key Communists—advocated a coalition to push for participation by the workers in the ongoing modernization of French society. Flexibility, these dissidents argued, was more important under the changed economic and social circumstances than was the continuation of a rigid antimanagement, pro-proletarian position on the part of the PCF. Insisting on the continuing validity of old theories of the inevitable impoverishment of the workers in a capitalist system, Thorez rejected PCF participation in the economic modernization movement and condemned those Communist leaders who had advocated such participation. As a consequence, the Communist-controlled trade union lost much of its following because of its cynical use of economic unrest for political purposes.

Thorez also was confronted with considerable opposition within the PCF to his position on the Algerian conflict. Some of his subordinates argued that the party should press more vigorously for Algerian independence and that the doctrines of Mao Tse-tung were more applicable than those of Khrushchev to the Algerian problem. Thorez was hesitant to accept these guidelines for two principal reasons. First, its trade-union element was opposed to a pro-Algerian position. Second, the Party wanted to avoid proscription at all costs.

While Thorez remained as skillful as ever at adapting the French line on various foreign policy issues to the shifts in Moscow's own foreign policy pronouncements, he apparently was not entirely successful in applying a similar flexibility to his approach to current domestic problems. While his counterpart, Togliatti, was encouraging open debate within the Italian Communist Party on foreign and domestic questions, Thorez was resorting for the most part to Stalinistic disciplinary measures—including purges—to keep his followers in line. He successfully weathered several attempts at resistance by the Party minority on certain policy issues.

By 1961, a number of key PCF leaders who had opposed Thorez's rigid approach to the new problems facing the party had either left the organization of their own volition or had been purged. Among those expelled were: Jean Baby, who had published a scathing criticism of the inadequacy of the continued conservative and inflexible approach of the PCF to meet the changing demands of the environment in which it now had to operate; Marcel Servin, a member of the Central Committee of the PCF since 1948 and formerly a close associate of Thorez; and Laurent Casanova, long-time leader of party activities among the French intellectuals.

Following the purge of these and other dissidents, the party hierarchy was reorganized. To forestall a succession crisis and to conpensate for Thorez's poor health, Waldeck-Rochet, long responsible for Communist activities among the French peasants, was elevated to the newly created post of Deputy Secretary-General of the PCF. Moscow-trained, like Thorez, Waldeck-Rochet was only five years younger than the late Secretary-General. Since his succession to the Secretary-Generalship following Thorez's demise, Waldeck-Rochet has continued to try to rule the party along the same relatively rigid, highly disciplined lines Thorez preferred during his own lifetime.

In France, then, iron-bound discipline and a tight organization of the Stalinist variety have remained the key approach to solving the problems of effective operation of the party. The unquestioned adherence of lower echelons to the rulings delivered by the Central Committee is still expected. Splinter groups have sprung up outside the party, and several pro-Chinese and anti-PCF publications have appeared, but these developments have not had a significant impact. The rank and file which votes Communist at the polls does not seem to have been significantly affected by the growing ideological dissent. Still concentrating primarily on the favorable image created by Thorez, this rank and file continues to identify with the PCF as the principal champion of its grievances.

The 1965 Presidential elections in France indicated that even the PCF, vigorous supporter of Moscow in the earlier test over the convening of an international Conference of Communist Parties, now has begun to tailor its activities to its own—not Moscow's—assessment of domestic requirements. The election indicated that the PCF has become perturbed over the cavalier treatment it received from Moscow during the debates on de-Stalizination and now is increasingly inclined to accept the guidelines for semi-autonomy set down in Togliatti's posthumously published "testament." While the USSR, in 1965, was tacitly supporting the candidacy of de Gaulle, the PCF was, through its candidate (François Mitterand), ruthlessly fighting against the incumbent. The net result was a loss of prestige for de Gaulle and a run-off election pitting him against the PCF-supported candidate. Although the PCF was somewhat slower than the counterpart Italian Communist Party to declare its independence of Moscow, at least a partial declaration of independence seemed in the offing.

The PCF clearly is undergoing a period of significant transition. Given the concomitant policy uncertainties which now are manifesting themselves, the question arises: Can the PCF continue to perpetuate its revolutionary image in the future? Most of the PCF leaders today are sixty or older; eventually younger persons will have to be assimilated into the party elite. The difficulties the PCF has experienced in recent years with a key youth organization, the Union des Étudiants Communistes de France (UEC), do not augur well for its prospects if Stalinistic rigidity is not entirely abandoned.

The UEC was formed approximately a decade ago in the midst of the dual debate over the implications of de-Stalinization and the preferred PCF position on support for the French rebels in Algeria. From the outset, the UEC has questioned the policies of the "old guard" party leadership. Gradually three factions emerged within this student organization: The first is a pro-Chinese group. A second group has been strongly influenced by Togliatti's ideas on "polycentrism," and it believes in a "French road to socialism" involving accommodation with domestic non-Communist leftist parties. A third group remains loyal to the PCF leadership. Even the "pro-party" faction of the UEC consistently has advocated greater autonomy for the student organization. All three factions have questioned the traditional dependence of Communist youth organizations on the parent party for establishing a "general line" and for furnishing political guidance.

The most serious crisis between the UEC and the PCF occurred between January 1963 and March 1965. In 1963, at its Sixth Congress, the UEC adopted a program constituting a political analysis different from the one contained in contemporary party theses. Despite requests from the PCF leaders, the UEC refused to withdraw this program from debate. Discussion stimulated by this confrontation soon prompted spokesmen for the UEC to argue that the party sought to curb discussion of its policies at the grass roots and that party leaders lacked the resiliency essential to guaranteeing a continuing impact on French society. Finally, they argued that the almost sacred tenet of the Third Comintern Congress concerning the subordination of all student organizations to the discipline of the Party was open to question. There were even some demands that the UEC become an "autonomous" Communist organization outside the political control of the PCF.

At its Seventh Congress in 1964, the UEC reaffirmed its right of free discussion unhampered by party discipline. An extraordinary Congress was scheduled for later in the year to take final action on the future relation of the UEC to the PCF. The PCF leadership saw to it that this special Congress was postponed until party control over the UEC delegates could be regained. By such tactics as exerting pressures on the regional student associations that elected delegates to the UEC, the PCF sought to "pack" the UEC with pro-Party members. In January 1965, the UEC national leaders published an open letter condemning the Party leadership for its use of pressure tactics and deploring, in general, its excessively Stalinist methods. In February, although the UEC's open letter had been attacked by the PCF leaders, a group of prominent Communist intellectuals published a document supporting the UEC position. Again, the PCF leaders condemned this critique of prevailing party practices.

Ultimately, in March 1965, the Eighth Congress of the UEC was held. Although the PCF had succeeded by this time in gaining control over about two-thirds of the UEC delegates, the sessions were stormy. Nevertheless, the 1963 documents which had created the crisis between UEC and the PCF were replaced by new policy pronouncements reaffirming the traditional subordination of the student organization to the Party. No debate on political issues was permitted, and a new, pro-Party leadership was elected. But those advocating a wider role for the UEC in French Communist activities have not yet been purged from the organization. While Party control over the restive students has been temporarily reasserted, this control may indeed prove to be tenuous.

How long will the PCF be able to apply effectively what aptly has been termed "the organizational weapon" to the struggle between Stalinistic rigidity and increasing demands for adaptability and open-mindedness? Do the French Communists want to realize, in the here and now, those opportunities afforded by present developments in their country? Or will they eventually be content, like the late Thorez, perennially to advocate a "united front" while ostensibly awaiting the arrival of Russian troops to liberate them from their immediate tasks?

Future developments will answer these key questions. Meanwhile, it is appropriate to note that of all the Communist parties of Western Europe, the PCF has been one of the slowest to abandon Stalinistic rigid and inflexible policies. But even the degree of inflexibility remaining today constitutes a pattern *à la Russe:* CPR inroads into French communism remain very insignificant.

The Italian Communist Party

The most obvious impact of the Sino-Soviet dispute on the Italian Communist Party (PCI) has been to accelerate trends which appeared quite some time before the dispute became public: namely, giving more encouragement and momentum to the PCI's persistent goal of gaining greater autonomy within the Communist movement.[2] After all, it was Togliatti who coined the term "polycentrism." As a matter of fact, it was probably Togliatti who, more than any other Communist leader outside the Soviet Union, appreciated the real significance of the condemnation of Stalin by Khrushchev. It now seems clear that the late and brilliant Italian leader understood that the denigration of Stalin most certainly would undermine the authority of the Soviet Union over world communism.

The open ideological dispute between China and the USSR afforded the Italian Communist Party a greater opportunity to encourage a developing trend toward emphasizing its own objectives, determined by the local environment, and de-emphasizing the interests of the Soviet Union.[3] This is not to say that the Italian Party did not continue

[2] We do not intend to suggest that the dispute is the sole reason for the flexibility of the Italian Communist Party. The PCI has been a model of flexibility within the Communist movement, and this tendency was given much impetus following the denunciation of Stalin.

[3] Italian Communist leaders did not agree among themselves as to the preferred "local actions." Some, like Amendola, seem to have assumed the immediate collapse of the center-left. Others debated this issue vigorously. Even Amendola gradually shifted his position.

to agree philosophically with the Soviet Union on the major issues, but only that it was less willing to come down automatically on the side of the USSR.

The dispute over Khrushchev's attempt to call an international conference of Communist parties to debate the Sino-Soviet conflict is a major case in point. Indeed, the Italian Party obviously had a stake in seeing that the dispute was not settled either by compromise or by a decisive confrontation in which one or the other of the two Communist giants was defeated; any such development would almost certainly have reduced the Italian Party's ability to pursue its increasingly independent policy. And although the Italian Party continued to agree with the Soviet position on major issues and to disagree openly with the Chinese position, it nevertheless looked favorably upon the Chinese challenge to Soviet domination of the Communist world movement. The Italian Party wished to maintain the position that the Soviets now had to *ask* for support rather than to *demand* it.

Accordingly, the Italian Communists were opposed—on the grounds that no satisfactory solution was possible—to a conference of Communists to debate the dispute. This would appear to be the first significant example of the Italian Party's defiance of the Soviet Union on a key policy question.

The leadership of the PCI is relatively young when compared, for example, with the leadership of the French Communist Party. Below the highest echelons, the Italian Communist leaders are for the most part men ranging in age from the late thirties to the late forties. What these elements of the leadership aspire to most of all is power *now* in Italy. They want complete freedom of action from any other Communist power center in order to bring their policies into consonance with the realities of the Italian political scence. In fact, one faction of the Italian Communist leadership has actually come out in favor of a party of the Left which would include among its membership the Socialists and the Catholic Left, although such a coalition probably would face many obstacles. Nevertheless, it is significant that an element in the Party has begun to consider its future in these terms.

The proposal for a party of the Left was made by Giorgio Amendola, who argued that neither the Socialists nor the Communists had in fifty years been able to come up with a program which could win the support of Western Europe's working classes. And he believed it was unlikely that they would be able to formulate an acceptable program in the future.

As Amendola put it: "A political organization which has not reached its objectives in half a century, with the cooperation of three generations of militants, must seek the reasons for this failure and must know how to transform itself."[4]

It is quite clear that the Sino-Soviet dispute has in no way lessened Communist influence over the party or the electorate in Italy. Indeed, the PCI's membership and share of the vote have increased since the dispute began. The Italian Communist Party now has its highest membership (more than 1,600,000 members) since just after the war. In the local elections of 1964 it increased its vote. In the most recent local elections, held in June 1966, the Communists suffered slight losses. Even though the PCI had suffered small losses beginning in 1964, some commentators have interpreted these most recent election results as the first major setback for the Italian Communist Party.[5] However, only 5 million people went to the polls and it is difficult at this early date to assess the long-term significance of these new returns. The Communist vote in Italy still remains quite large.

It should also be noted that Italian President Guiseppe Saragat, leader of the Social Democrats and a long-time opponent of the Communists, was elected only because the Communists gave him their votes. They control one-fourth of the Italian vote and they dominate the largest labor union in Italy.

It is difficult to say now where all this will lead. Although the Italian Communist Party leadership is still searching for a coalition arrangement, it remains to be seen whether the membership will endorse any meaningful collaboration with other parties of the Left. Many of them may be too tradition-bound to accept such a novel

---

4 *Rinascita,* November 24, 1964.

5 For example, Lily Marx, writing in the *Rome Daily American* on July 6, 1966, stated: "The outstanding fact, apart from the clear vote of confidence received by the center left as a whole, is the success of the Social Democrats and the evidence of the difficulties the Communist Party is facing.

change in the PCI's approach.[6] And should the PCI leadership obtain the support of the party membership, the whole idea could founder on the fact that the other Left parties (the Socialist and the Catholic Left) may not join with them. Still, the political spectrum in Italy is weighted heavily to the Left, and the policy advocated by the Italian Party leadership is consistent with the developing realities of the Italian political environment.

If the Italian Communist Party should be able to join with the majority of the non-Communist Italian Left, it is quite possible that its vote-getting capacity—always potent but long inhibited by the Party's adherence to Moscow's direction—will be enhanced. It is not unlikely that the PCI in union with the other parties of the Left—parties which may be more divided among themselves than the Communists—would dominate any such coalition arrangement.

In large measure, this may be the most significant impact of the Sino-Soviet dispute as it relates to the Italian Communist Party. The dispute has opened for the PCI the opportunity to become a more open and thus a more traditional Western political party within the Italian political arena, at least creating the possibility that it may seek common cause with the traditional parties of the Italian Left.

It might be added that the PCI has always been considered the best financed and best led Communist Party in the free world. It is still well financed, largely through its own local arrangements and techniques. And the present leadership, while perhaps not as brilliant and adroit as Togliatti, seems still more than adequate to the task of perpetuating the influential power position which the PCI has achieved in Italian politics.

French and Italian Party Policies

In general, most of the West European Communist parties have achieved a new independence as a consequence of the Sino-Soviet

[6] And there is no intent here to suggest that the leadership sees eye-to-eye on this issue. A faction led by Ingrao still believes in a more rigid adherence to a traditional Communist policy. But the bulk of the PCI has followed the Longo-Amendola approach—making the PCI into a more open and thus a more traditional and a more respectable party.

dispute. It has given them an increasing capability for pursuing policies more closely tailored to their own political environments than did their previous relationships with Moscow. (These previous relationships involved, in essence, Soviet domination of their domestic and foreign policies.) It is, perhaps, the French Communist Party which, partially because of its internal structure and its traditionalism, has been the most reluctant of the West European parties to exploit the Sino-Soviet dispute to its own domestic advantage.

For the Italian Communists, the dispute has given impetus to trends already evident—trends toward a much more independent policy, a policy much in line with the prevailing Italian political climate. Domestically, these trends have involved an effort by the Party leadership to associate itself more directly with the Socialists and the Catholic Left and, in effect, to transform the PCI into something more closely resembling a conventional West European political party.

Unlike their Italian counterparts, the leaders of the PCF have resisted debate and dissension within their party and within its satellite mass organizations. Stalinistic purges have occurred in France; in Italy, intra-Party debate has been more commonplace.

The Italian Party today is increasingly interested in achieving national power as quickly as possible, and some of its leaders see little hope of doing so as a classical Communist Party. The Italian Communists have little interest in waiting any longer for the revolution of the Italian proletariat. By contrast, the French Party leaders still seem to await the day when a shift in the balance of power in Europe will permit them to exploit classical "revolutionary opportunities." However, even the French Communists are becoming impatient, as their support for François Mitterand in the last Presidential election demonstrated. (Moscow lent ostensible support to de Gaulle.)

The Italian Party is extremely disillusioned with the prospects of achieving world communism in the traditional sense. Dissidents within the French Communist Party have expressed similar disillusionments. Nevertheless, the leaders of the French Party appear more reluctant to adapt doctrine to changed environmental conditions. Only since the recent Presidential electoral campaign have they begun to show the first signs of flexibility.

The Italian Party, then, has been more resilient in its effort to adjust to an increasingly complex international environment not predicted by Marx, Engels, Lenin, or Stalin. In fact, despite occasional vigorous opposition to his policies, one of Togliatti's consistently great skills was his ability to adjust the Italian Party's policies to meet local requirements without alienating Moscow. The French Party has accepted post-Stalinist Soviet innovations reluctantly and still lags behind in introducing changes in doctrine and in practice.

Neither the PCI nor the PCF any longer fully acknowledges the right of Moscow to dictate their policies. An example of the different approaches of the two parties to their relations with the CPSU is the Italian Party's boldness in openly refusing to endorse Moscow's proposal for a conference to reconcile differences with the CPR—as contrasted with the French Party's support of Moscow on the importance of such a conference.

Neither the PCI nor the PCF—nor any other majority element within the West European Communist movement—has adopted a pro-Chinese position. While splinter groups exist in Western Europe, to date their influence has been minimal. The principal effect of the Sino-Soviet dispute on the West European Communist parties, then, has been to continue the trend toward the modification of their relations with Moscow—a trend which dramatically began with Khrushchev's secret speech at the Twentieth Party Congress.

Asia

3. China's Fortunes in Asia

—*ABRAHAM M. HALPERN*

The Chinese Communists over the past five years have used their assets with great intelligence and have been able to score important political successes in many Asian countries. This is a noteworthy accomplishment, especially because of the initial weaknesses in their position.

The Asian Communist World

The success of the Chinese Communists is particularly evident in their relations with other Communist parties in Asia. In early 1961, immediately after the Moscow Conference of 1960, the Chinese position appeared weak and there seemed to be a real danger that they might find themselves isolated within the bloc and therefore susceptible to Soviet pressure. Since then they have succeeded in constructing what looks like a rather firm coalition of parties and splinter parties which support the Chinese position on matters in dispute within the bloc.

This coalition is not an empire. It is based not on absolute Chinese domination of other parties but on coincidences of interest. Therefore the coalition is not necessarily eternal. Furthermore, in some ways it may place certain limits on Chinese Communist action. Having assumed a position of leadership, the Chinese may find, as others have found before them, that a leader occasionally can remain a leader only by deferring to his followers.

A Historic Review

Close relations between the Chinese Communist parties and other Asian parties go back in some cases quite far. Some of the smaller Asian parties—like those of Malaysia, Burma, and Thailand—have been closer to the Chinese than to the Soviets, at least since the Communist victory in China in 1949. The Japanese Communist Party had important cooperative relations with the Chinese during World War II and in the period from 1950 to 1955, when some of its top leaders used Peking as an asylum and a base for directing the strategy of their party at home. The Japanese Communist Party, however, has always been torn between the influence of Moscow and Peking and only in the last few years has it definitely aligned itself with Peking.

In early 1955 the Soviets adopted a formula which described the Communist world as being under the double leadership of the Soviet Union and the Chinese People's Republic. This probably reflected an intention to allow China a substantially independent sphere of influence in Asia, at least in dealing with Asian countries on the state level (though less clearly in dealing with other Asians on the party level). When differences arose between the Soviet and the Chinese Parties in connection with the positions taken at the Twentieth Congress of the CPSU in 1956, only the Chinese Party seemed to be strongly affected and to be able to take an independent line. It is worth remembering, however, that after the Twentieth Congress many leaders of other Asian parties stopped in China on their way home and spent enough time there to indicate serious discussions.

Moscow did not strongly reassert itself in Asia until early in 1960—that is to say, after the critical point in the Sino-Soviet dispute had been reached. This point was signaled by Khrushchev's visit to Peking in October 1959, immediately after his visit to the United States. Soon after it became clear that there was an extremely serious difference of views between the Soviets and the Chinese on the question of strategy and tactics in dealing with the West.

The major moves made by the Chinese in their relations with the Communist regimes in North Korea and North Vietnam and with other Asian Communist parties began after the 1960 Moscow Conference. In July 1961, China and North Korea concluded a treaty almost identical to the Soviet—North Korean treaty of the same month, but one which implied a greater depth of mutual commitment between China and North Korea than the Soviets were willing to undertake. The tactics subsequently used by the Chinese were to raise a series of issues in such a way that other Asian parties had to declare themselves on these issues no matter how reluctant they might be to acknowledge a dispute within the world movement or to do anything that would widen the split.

During and after the Twenty-second Congress of the CPSU in late 1961, the Chinese used Khrushchev's attack on Albania to pose the issue of national independence and were supported in various degrees by most of the Asian parties. Their biggest windfall was the Cuban incident of October 1962, which they pressed for all it was worth and on which again they obtained significant support from other Asians. Their grievances against the Soviet Union for its position on the Sino-Indian dispute constituted a less effective but nevertheless useful issue of this kind. In mid-1962, at the World Peace Council meeting of that year, the Chinese drew the issue of nuclear proliferation in quite clear terms even though this meant reversing their earlier stand on the value of a nuclear test ban. The groundwork was thereby laid for the position which the Chinese took when the test ban treaty was concluded in July 1963. The treaty was the supreme issue in the Chinese design for making Asian parties declare themselves; and by the time the issue arose, the Chinese could be certain that they would receive widespread support among Asian Communists. The pattern continued in connection with the Chinese detonation of a nuclear device in October 1964.

Shortly after the Cuban incident, it became quite evident that the major single target of the Chinese in the world movement was Khrushchev, his general strategy, and particularly his strategy for putting pressure on the Chinese. Chinese behavior at European party congresses at the end of 1962 and in the early part of 1963, as well as their intransigent position in international front organizations from 1963 on, made sense only on the assumption that they thought Khrushchev could be overthrown. His ouster in October 1964 was not the result of Chinese activities alone, or even primarily of Chinese pressure. But his handling of the Chinese was clearly considered a major problem, and his downfall was at the least a demonstration of the strength of the Chinese position within the bloc.

By that time, the negative effects of the Sino-Soviet dispute on Russia's position had become evident. Chinese strength has been demonstrated by the coolness with which the Chinese leadership has responded to the approaches of Kosygin and Brezhnev, whose aims seem to be limited for the present to reducing the disadvantages they suffer from a continuation of the Sino-Soviet dispute rather than to moving rapidly toward the restructuring of a tightly organized bloc or world movement.

Conditions for Success

North Korea and North Vietnam

Success such as the Chinese have scored must be based on favorable conditions intelligently exploited.

In regard to North Korea and North Vietnam, the following appear to be some of the important conditions that had already existed. First, these two regimes shared with other Communist regimes a general trend toward national communism and toward independence from central dictation. North Korea had been moving in this direction and also moving closer to China since 1958, when Kim Il Sung eliminated the last of his important rivals and consolidated his dictatorial powers within North Korea. Both North Korea and North Vietnam shared to some extent China's doubts concerning the approach Khrushchev made to the United States in 1959. Like China, they had demands which would not be satisfied by an accommodation based on the status quo in Asia and which they did not want to leave to the Soviets to bargain away in their name.

Their major demand had to do with the unification of their countries. This goal is not something dictated by the Chinese, but something to which North Korea and North Vietnam are deeply attached. China was willing to lend more support to their demands than the Soviets appeared to be, and certainly China gave no appearance of wanting to use their situations as counters in bargaining with the United States for its own advantage. In both these cases, then, the growth of Chinese military power, including nuclear capability, is a favorable factor in the balance; whereas, to the Soviet Union it implies many dangers.

Finally, China has in the last few years given significant economic assistance to both regimes. The economic programs to which North Korea and North Vietnam are now committed could be more easily integrated with China's economic program than with that of the Soviet Union.

On the basis of this kind of common interest, the three Asian Communist regimes have developed a quite effective working alliance and have coordinated many aspects of their foreign relations, including their relations with countries of the Third World. The common interests of the Chinese Communist Party with nonruling parties elsewhere in Asia are less extensive and less profound.

Japan

In the Japanese Communist Party (JCP) in the last few years a large group of second echelon leaders has emerged, many of whom received their training in China and have no important ties with the CPSU. This group is sometimes referred to by the Japanese as the young officers corps and is thought to play a role somewhat like that of the field grade officers group in the Japanese Army before World War II. In other words, these young leaders have considerably more power to determine the decisions of their superiors than their formal rank implies.

The JCP program does not anticipate a direct drive for power in the near future. Its short-term aim is to promote anti-Americanism with the specific objective of creating sharp political issues in 1970 when the existing United States—Japan Security Treaty may be subject to revision. Its longer range aim is to carry out organizational activities and "education," looking toward the day when a direct drive for power may come to be a feasible proposition. For these purposes the JCP believes that its posture must be a strongly militant one. This posture is closer to that of the CCP than of the CPSU. De-Stalinization as practiced by Khrushchev had to be repudiated by a party situated as the JCP is, and the defections and splits which resulted had to be accepted as a necessary price.

Indonesia

Before the Communist reversal in Indonesia in early 1966, the domestic position and objectives of the Indonesian Party (PKI) were quite different from those of the JCP. A much larger party, it had a wider scope for organizational activities outside its own ranks, and was closer than the JCP to a position of bidding seriously for power. Its basic strategy was until recently to cooperate with the existing government rather than to attack it; but at the same time its hope had been to influence the existing government in the direction of a more and more anti-Western and pro-Communist position.

Superficially PKI strategy seemed closer to the Soviet than to the Chinese posture, but this appearance was misleading. The Chinese knew a great deal about tactical flexibility and there was nothing to indicate that they disapproved of the PKI strategy. At the same time, the PKI continued to seek not just power alone but eventually a monopoly of power, strictly observing the Chinese view of the importance of maintaining autonomy and separateness exactly at the time when it was most actively cooperating with non-Communist allies. The PKI thus had a definite interest in maintaining a militant posture and avoiding a dilution of its ideology. It also regarded de-Stalinization as unfavorable to the maintenance of its integrity as an organization and had good reasons—as did North Korea and North Vietnam or the JCP—for following the strictly anti-imperialist line enunciated by the Chinese.

India, Ceylon, and Australia

In several cases in Asia the Sino-Soviet dispute resulted in splits within the existing Communist parties: for example, in the Indian and Ceylonese Parties as well as the Australian Party. A potential split was inherent in the composition and domestic position of each of the parties concerned. The pro-Chinese splinter in each case obtains some tactical satisfaction as well as some disadvantages. In relation to issues between the CCP and CPSU, these splits have in all cases constituted a net gain for the CCP and a net loss for the CPSU. For example, these splits added to the difficulties faced by the CPSU in trying to convene a new world meeting of Communist parties against the opposition of the CCP.

The Soviet Union and Asian Communism

It has been stated above that the Asian Communist coalition is not necessarily permanent. The Soviet Union has some ability to undercut the bases of the coalition but at the present time does not appear to be in a strong position to do so. It would have to offer the equivalent of what the Chinese offer; and to make this offer would involve a reversal of some general trends of Soviet policy toward the West. The Soviet dilemma seems to be that it can affect the solidarity of the Asian Communist coalition only by loosening the total structure of world communism (that is, by supporting national Communist tendencies) rather than by tightening that structure.

The Chinese Peoples Republic and Non-Communist Asia

The success of the CPR in its relations with non-Communist Asian countries following the Sino-Soviet split can be rather simply measured. For many years, particularly since the Korean war, the CPR has claimed that no problem in Asia can be solved without its participation. That claim now seems to have a reality that it did not have when first made.

The Chinese have succeeded especially in their relations with Cambodia and Pakistan and to a somewhat lesser extent in their relations with Japan. They claim to be operating in Asia in the 1955 Bandung spirit, but an important change has taken place in the last ten years. At the 1955 Bandung Conference the Chinese offered universal cooperation and mutual assistance to all Asian countries. At present they are playing the power politics game for all it is worth, which means discriminating sharply between friends and enemies. The contrast between their modesty at Bandung in 1955 and their present great-power pose is very marked.

Again, successes like these must be based on favorable conditions. One of these was the prestige the CPR acquired in many Asian eyes in 1949 by eliminating the foreign influences which had before then been important. Their prestige grew considerably during the war in Korea, which the Chinese, by ignoring the price they had to pay, can plausibly represent as a great victory for China.

Second, in much of Asia it has long been an article of faith that the Chinese would not be subservient to the Soviet Union for any length of time. The belief that the Chinese would make themselves independent at the earliest possible moment was usually justified by the view that the CCP was really a nationalist movement and that it would respond to deep cultural influences by displaying moderation rather than ideological rigidity. Despite the positions taken on ideological issues by the Chinese, the reaction to the split, not only in Asia but elsewhere, has characteristically been that it confirmed the original expectation. In a certain sense this is true, whatever the variations in ideology. As soon as the CPR adopted a foreign political posture independent of the Soviet Union, it began to some extent to operate in Asian relations as an autonomous national unity. Thus it became possible for other Asian nations either to find a modus vivendi with China or to recognize certain common objectives. In a few cases, particularly in the thinking of some Japanese, the split resulted in opening the way for a new but traditional calculation of China's world role. This calculation derived from the ancient principle of power politics—that when your enemies are divided you should support the weaker against the stronger. The principle is a traditional one, but it is questionable whether it applies in the modern context.

The critical point, however, seems to be that the CPR has something to offer to many Asian countries. What it can offer is in some cases rewards and in others punishment.

The rewards it can offer are political and are valuable to the extent that they are rewards that the United States cannot—at any rate, does not—offer. The CPR offers Cambodia protection against possible threats from Thailand, South Vietnam, and even North Vietnam, as well as a few direct economic benefits. It offers Indonesia at the least support for its demands against Malaysia and at the most the prospect of cooperation in dividing Asia into compatible spheres of influence. It offers Pakistan an anchor to windward at a time when Pakistan feels that the West is unnecessarily tipping the balance against Pakistan by strengthening India. Pakistan has further profited by its recent friendship with China by gaining flexibility in its foreign relations and prestige in succeeding India as a potential mediator of difficulties between China and the West. To isolationist Burma, China offers an approach which, in Burmese eyes, looks a good deal less like interference in Burma's affairs than anything the West has had to offer.

On the punishment side, China is free to take as hostile an attitude as it deems profitable toward, for example, Thailand, South Vietnam, and Malaysia.

In relation to Japan, the CPR is not in a strong position to offer either rewards or punishments. It can and has offered both, but in neither case can it achieve a great deal of credibility. Japan obtains no positive advantages in refraining from full normal relations with China; but on the other hand it has in substance most of what it wants by way of *de facto* relations and therefore does not lose much by the absence of formal diplomatic contacts. How long this will be true depends largely on the development of Japan's view of its proper role in the world.

4. The Communist Parties of Japan and India

—LUCIAN PYE

The Sino-Soviet split has drastically or subtly affected nearly every aspect of political life in Asia. It has been the most significant development for Asia since the Korean war and the original drawing of the lines of the cold war. There are many consequences of the dispute that are dramatic and fully manifest. There is much more, however, that is still latent, involving mainly the subtle changing of attitudes and outlooks which in time may be of the greatest significance.

The Drift Toward and then Away from Peking

It is not appropriate here to try to trace the details of the power struggle that eventually has forced all the Asian parties to choose sides, or to split into factions. The general picture has been one of the majority of Asian parties' first showing significant signs of support for Peking and then gradually pulling away. Thus in the spring of 1965, of the three Asian parties in power—North Vietnam, North

Korea, and Mongolia—only the last was fully on the side of the Russians. Of the fourteen other parties in Asia, eight appeared solidly on the side of Peking; in six countries there were strong pro-Chinese factions or splinter movements. A year later the trend was entirely in the opposite direction: by late spring 1966 both North Korea and North Vietnam had moved to a more neutral position, and the Chinese could claim domination only over the trivial parties of New Zealand, Thailand, and Malaysia. In short, in the first confusion provoked by the Sino-Soviet dispute, the Chinese initially scored the greatest successes in Asia, but in time they proved to lack staying power.

There was evidence as early as 1961 that the Russians realized that the trend might go against them in Asia. At the Twenty-second Congress of the CPSU (October 1961), when the Kremlin was mounting its heavy attack on Albania and thus indirectly on China, the Russians sought to keep the Asian parties from making any direct references to Chinese positions. By January of 1963 at the East German Party Congress, no Asian party was permitted to speak, except for the Japanese representative who gave only a moderately pro-Peking statement. Subsequently the North Koreans published what they had intended to say at the Congress: it was a strong attack on "revisionism" and a denial that "dogmatism" was the main issue for world communism.

The two major events which compelled the Asian parties to reconsider their relations to Peking and Moscow were: first, the increased American commitment to Vietnam; and, second, the coup d'état in Indonesia on September 30, 1965, which brought the army to power and brought about the complete destruction of the PKI, which was at the time the largest Communist party in the world out of power. Chinese setbacks in Africa and in Latin America also had their reverberations in Asia, causing all the Communist leaders to reconsider the likelihood of Peking representing the "wave of the future."

It is worth considering the reasons why the Chinese had their apparent early successes because some of these may again in the future affect the feelings of Asian Communists toward both Peking and Moscow.

First, the mood of Asia is revolutionary, and thus the Chinese spirit of urging on "wars of liberation" is psychologically appealing even if it may not be tactically feasible in all countries.

Second, the Soviet appeal for "peaceful coexistence" seems to suggest the acceptance of, if not complete surrender to, the forces of "imperialism." Asian parties are not prepared to give up the theme of militant anti-Americanism—the only theme which, in a sense, puts them in the big league of world politics.

Third, the Chinese have been assisted by latent racial and cultural sentiments. Moscow is European in the eyes of most Asians, while Peking represents the triumph of a once poor and backward Asian people.

Finally, within the logic of traditional Marxism-Leninism the Chinese have had most of the arguments on their side. Therefore, to appreciate the Russian position it is necessary to take into account non-ideological considerations—such as the dangers of thermonuclear war—about which the Asian parties are relatively less concerned.

As significant as such general issues may have been, it is important to recognize that each Asian party had its particular reasons for taking its position, and these differed greatly from case to case. This is an extremely important point for policy planning. For in spite of the nearly uniform drift first toward and then away from Peking, there has not been a common pattern; and Peking's successes and failures do not rest on the application of any single formula.

The Japanese Communist Party

Indeed, in terms of the logic of the fundamental positions of both Moscow and Peking, it would be hard to explain why the Japanese Communist Party so quickly became so strongly pro-Peking and even engaged with Moscow in a private polemic unrelated to the Sino-Soviet dispute.

Japan is not an underdeveloped country and a strategy of "wars of national liberation" makes no sense in the Japanese context. On the contrary, given the pacifist sentiments of the country and the Japanese horror of the atomic bomb, it would be more logical and appropriate for the Japanese Communists to champion a strategy of "peaceful coexistence." In fact, however, the initial reflex of the Japanese Communist Party was to defy all such tactical considerations and to come out strongly for Peking and even to denounce the partial test ban treaty.

The Japanese Communists arrived at their initial decision in part because of the personal ties of some of their leaders with leading Chinese figures, and in part because of the ineptness of the Russians in dealing with visiting Japanese delegations and their clumsiness in seeking to support a splinter, pro-Moscow party.

Even more important, however, is the fundamental fact that if the Japanese Communists were to be denied the issue of anti-Americanism and were forced to support the spirit of détente between Russia and the United States, they would be completely undercut from all sides within the arena of Japanese politics. A policy of supporting the Russian view of world conditions would make the Japanese Communists a pale copy of the left-wing Socialists. In short, the peculiar configuration of Japanese domestic politics helps explain in large measure why the Japanese party has reacted as it did to the Sino-Soviet dispute.

Although the Japanese Communist leaders found it expedient at first to identify with Peking, gradually during 1965 and early 1966 they were compelled to adopt a more reserved position. As the Chinese continued to make further tests in the nuclear area, and as the Japanese population experienced the realities of the fallout from these tests, it became increasingly embarrassing politically for the Japanese Communists to show unreserved support for Peking.

The Indian Communist Party

Similarly in the Indian case, local and, even more important, intraparty considerations have heavily influenced their response to the dispute—which has been one of seriously splitting the Communist Party of India. The CPI had about 250,000 members and was the largest opposition party to the Congress Party, gaining about 11 million votes in the 1962 elections (which was, however, only about 10 per cent of the total).

In the face of the Chinese suppression of the Tibetan revolt and their subsequent attack on the Indian borders, and in light of the degree of assistance Moscow has given to India in recent years, it might seem implausible that there would be many Indians prepared to identify themselves publicly in support of Peking. Yet as late as the fall of 1965 a substantial and, in some areas, predominant fraction of the Indian Communists were pro-Chinese.

Indeed, the pro-Peking leaders, most of whom were being detained in jail without trial by the Indian Government, won the largest number of seats of any party in the Kerala state elections in 1965.

The extraordinary fact that a party committed to a foreign foe—and a foe that had gone so far as to humiliate one's nation in a test of arms—could still be a dynamic political force was in part a reflection of the degree of demoralization and restlessness characteristic of certain segments of the Indian population.

Hence it would be incorrect to view the political struggle within the Communist movement entirely in terms of the clash between the policies of Moscow and Peking. In fact, the division within the CPI antedated the Sino-Soviet split. The crack in the monolithic structure of international communism made factionalism more acceptable among the Indian Communists, but the impetus for division of the CPI was largely indigenously inspired. A clash of personalities within the CPI was given a solid power base by the natural division of the CPI into its national level and some very substantial local and regional organizations. This structural division was reinforced by a fundamental ideological cleavage that struck at the heart of a basic ambivalence of Communist movements in the underdeveloped areas.

The national leadership, in the spirit of the current Moscow approach, sees the need for a broad nationalist approach tactically involving alliances with liberal bourgeois and petit bourgeois elements in opposing "imperalism" and "international capitalism." In short, they believe the advance of communism can best be realized by working on the conflicting forces within Congress so as to strengthen the left against the moderates and to isolate the right. What is now the pro-Peking element of the CPI insists, on the other hand, that the situation calls for more intense class warfare leading to a full social revolution.

Thus, as in the case of Japan, the domestic political situation in India initially put a squeeze on the more moderate, pro-Moscow elements and favored the more radical elements who could thus be an unambiguous pole. Also, however, as in the case of Japan, the trend in domestic political developments in India during 1965 and 1966 compelled a reversal in the position of the Communists. The war against Pakistan brought about a spirit of war fever and, even more important, it gave the Indians a degree of self-confidence which greatly reduced the appeals of the more radical pro-Peking faction. The pro-Peking Communists found that by identifying both with China and Pakistan they had become too obviously associated with the enemies of Indian nationalism.

The Sino-Soviet Split: Complicating Relations

In viewing how domestic political considerations in at least two Asian countries have affected the alignment of the Asian Communist parties, we have carried our analysis over to the realm of the Sino-Soviet split's influence on national politics and the foreign-policy orientations of the Asian states.

In this larger context, the major conclusion to be drawn is that the split has dramatically shattered the relatively neat and clear-cut pattern of three dominant foreign-policy orientations: Communist, pro-Western, and nationalist. In the somewhat more fluid situation which now exists, there are considerably more alternatives; and governments will tend to make more complex calculations as to where their particular national interests lie.

The Asian states are entering a period in which they will feel much more individualistic needs for security. Thus, while the Sino-Soviet split has made it easier for India to move to a position of confrontation against China, it has also created a situation which will certainly bring Pakistan into closer association with China.

At the other end of Asia we find that Japan must also cope with a more complex world as a consequence of the Sino-Soviet split. It will no longer be possible for the Japanese in formulating foreign policy to feel that they can simplify their alternatives to mere reactions to American policies. All varieties of Japanese politicians will find that dogmatic postures are no longer possible and that the country must find its own individual position in relation to the whole range of Asian states as well as to the United States and Russia.

Some Common Consequences

The effects of the Sino-Soviet split common to the Asian states in general might be noted: First, it seems that the Sino-Soviet split is profound and that it has already created some permanent changes in Communist politics in Asia and in Asian relations in general. Radical politics will continue to be strong in Asia, but will not be played out under the assumption that ultimately there can be only one true understanding of communism. As factions develop and national Communist leaders commit themselves to different positions, it will become increasingly difficult to reestablish the unity of communism regardless of the course of Russian-Chinese relations.

Second, as a consequence of the Sino-Soviet dispute, all the Communist leaders, as well as national leaders, must now make their decisions in the face of much stronger cross pressures. Even the strongest pro-Peking leaders can see the advantages of not losing all their independence: Hanoi, for example, has found it essential to move away from the close embrace of Peking and to find a position between Peking and Moscow.

Third, the unfolding situation means that there is a greater possibility for initiative and vigorous policies by all parties at all levels of Asian politics. Indeed, the very need for greater adroitness also means that there will be greater payoffs for taking dynamic initiatives.

Finally although some of the problems and dangers in Asia have receded, the unfolding situations will pose new problems and dangers for the United States. In time, Asia will pass through this period of transition which has followed from the disrupting consequences of the Sino-Soviet split. Eventually new patterns of relations, both between the Communists and their domestic rivals and among the Asian states themselves, are certain to emerge. If the United States can conduct its policies with imagination and can provide guidance and leadership in establishing such a new order, then the ultimately beneficial effects of the Sino-Soviet split will be fully realized. For the destruction of the myth and of the practices of monolithic communism is certainly one of the most optimistic turns in world history.

Africa

5. Background on Communism in Africa

—*WILLIAM E. GRIFFITH*

Communism came to Africa from Europe along with European culture and politics. Africa's Communist parties and groups were originally established by Europeans and they have long remained multiracial. But like other European political movements, they have never obtained any serious mass support from the Africans. The Marxist-Leninist emphases on the proletariat, on multiracial internationalism, and on atheism have always run contrary to African traditions and culture. The few Western-educated intellectuals who have become Communists have been preoccupied with, when not suppressed by, the rising wave of anticolonialism and radical pan-African nationalism which characterizes the new, modernizing African intelligentsia.

To most black Africans the Russians are as European as any other whites; moreover, Russian manipulation of European and African Communist parties and groups for purely Soviet purposes soon disillusioned most of the early African sympathizers.[1] Furthermore, the (ostensibly) rationalist ideology of Marxism-Leninism, or indeed any political

[1]George Padmore, *Pan-Africanism or Communism?* (New York: Roy, 1956).

ideology, had little appeal to any but the most Westernized Africans, who—as was most strikingly shown by the severance in the early 1950s by the *Rassemblement démocratique africaine* (RDA) of its ties with French communism—were fully prepared to give lip service to Communist ideological and policy formulas that served their purposes, only to abandon them when that seemed more in accord with their interests.

Qualifying Communism for Africa

Africans tend to be undogmatic and pragmatic and to prefer the achievement of consensus to prolonged ideological struggle. South of the Sahara and even in North Africa, therefore, political theories and ideologies mean much less than north of the Mediterranean. Those African intellectuals and radical leaders who have been influenced by Marxism-Leninism have been attracted first by its organizational aspects and then by such general Marxist-Leninist concepts as state ownership and control of the economy and economic determinism, which they see as simultaneously allowing a recovery of pre-industrial communal virtues and a modernization by means of industrialization. Most of them have not accepted Marxism's hostility to religion, its stress on the "leading role of the working class," or the belief in the necessity of an elite urban proletariat rather than a mass party oriented toward the peasantry. (This last exclusion makes particularly clear the preference of many radical Africans for Chinese, as opposed to Soviet, policy positions.) Finally, some radical African nationalist leaders influenced by Marxist-Leninist concepts (particularly those in Guinea and Mali) probably have thought of themselves (as Castro in all likelihood does) as Marxist-Leninists who have successfully adapted the best of that doctrine to their national circumstances.

Indeed they may even have envisioned the Russians and the Chinese as also trying to adapt ideological Marxism to specific conditions, thereby contributing to a looser, more permissive current in the international Communist movement than that which existed previously. Such thinking was further encouraged by the Sino-Soviet split itself as it conduced all Communist parties toward differentiation.

It is true that some African students who were fed strong doses of leftist (including Communist) ideology while being educated in London or Paris in the 1940s and 1950s retained a liking for both Communist terminology and its organizational aspects. Moreover, the organizational aspect continued to attract them via leftwing trade union channels in Africa. For these young African intellectuals, however, Communism was primarily a method of rapid modernization; of the establishment, organization, and discipline of a contemporary, intellectual African elite; and of obtaining aid from Communist states.

Thus state ownership and central planning, the Leninist model of one-party organization, and economic and sometimes political ties with the Soviet Union remained characteristic of some of the newer African states, notably Guinea, Ghana, and Mali. (This was not the first time that the organizational aspects of Leninism had outlived the rest of its ideology; the same thing happened with the Kuomintang after 1927.) When in 1961 Soviet meddling and some native intellectual communism appeared to Sekou Touré to be menacing his control of Guinea, he struck fast and ruthlessly to crush dissidence at home and return to a neutralist posture abroad, while keeping (as did Chiang Kai-shek in 1927) the Leninist organizational and economic model for his own one-party state.

In 1965 in Ghana the Convention Peoples Party (CPP) had at least as many features of fascism as communism.[2] Indeed, the prevalence of Marxist rather than Fascist doctrine in Africa stems from the fact that the European colonizing powers were largely anti-Communist—as a result of which the anticolonialist Africans were naturally attracted to the enemy of their enemy, the Soviets. (Had the Italian Facists not been colonialists in Africa, and the Nazis clearly desirous of becoming colonialists, the same kind of attraction might have held true for fascism—as indeed it did for so many Arabs in the Middle East.)

---

[2]Walter Kolarz, "The West African Scene," *Problems of Communism* (November-December 1961), pp. 15-24.

Pan-Africanism

The primary focus of the African elites—pan-African nationalism—did not derive from communism. Being modernizers and thus determined to depose the traditional African tribal elites, the new elites could not base their power upon the tribes; on the other hand, the colonial boundaries were creations of the colonizers and could thus only with difficulty serve as their rallying symbol for modernization and independence. The goal of a united black Africa was the result. In turn, pan-Africanism plus modernization led to such general concepts as "African socialism"[3]—a varying mixture of Marxism and utopian socialism combined with African attitudes of consensus, the charismatic concept of the tribal chieftain, common ownership of land and property, and extended family.

Realistically, pan-Africanism made as little actual political progress as have "pan-" movements in other areas of the world. Disillusioned, the modernizing elite turned their focus to nation-building within their own states, artificial and colonial as their boundaries were. Only radical African leaders such as Nkrumah and Sekou Touré, who effectively established supremacy over traditionalist tribal elements, could afford to spend much energy on pan-Africanist political activity.

However, although on the whole pan-Africanism remains a powerful albeit frustrated dream and rallying point, it and the present African rulers also stand as the major obstacles to Soviet and Chinese ambitions in Africa. For the desire to form a coalition strong enough to keep Africa out of the cold war is an integral part of the drive for pan-African unity. This nearly unanimous African objective not to become the pawn of either Western or Communist interests evolved from the African states' experience in the United Nations. Undeniably, the radical African elites greatly feared what they considered the dangers of continued, if indirect (i.e., economic), domination by the ex-colonial powers. "Neo-colonialism" is still a persistent cry.

---

[3]William H. Friedland and Carl G. Rosberg, Jr., Eds., *African Socialism* (Stanford: Stanford University Press, 1964); Special Issue on African Socialism, *Africa Report* (May 1963), especially Ruth Schachter Morgenthau, "African Socialism: Declaration of Ideological Independence," pp. 3-7.

Yet the Soviets several times overplayed their hand, most notably in Guinea and the Congo, and the Chinese did the same in Malawi. Most African leaders therefore have learned not only the danger of letting Communist as well as European powers go too far in Africa but also, and more importantly, how relatively easy it is to outplay the Communists at their own game. On the other hand, there does remain one area of potentially serious Communist penetration within the modernizing sectors of African society. The success of some African states in secondary and higher education (contrasted with a slowness in economic development) has produced rising numbers of "academic proletarians," who desire the power and privileges of the post-independence elite. They are attracted to the Communist model of rapid modernization in the hands of new, disciplined intelligentsia and furnish an increasing base for Soviet and Chinese influence.

A Basic Perspective

Before one begins an analysis of Communist activities in Africa, the following important but often neglected preliminary points should be considered. First, although the number, size and significance of Communist parties and groups in Africa is very limited, the influence and activities of Communist states there is much more significant. Futhermore, Communist influence is increasingly exercised not through disciplined Communist individuals or groups but rather through radical African nationalist movements.

Second, in the context of the radical nationalist movements, African politics is carried on by blacks and whites, but it cannot be accurately portrayed as such a dichotomy. For the extent to which radical African nationalists may come under Communist influence hinges in large part upon how long their goals have been frustrated, the depth of their impatience with a lack of victory, and their inability to find support elsewhere.

Yet, thirdly, the temptation of the radical African nationalists to turn to the Communist powers for aid has been blunted by the Sino-Soviet rift. This dispute has given the Africans a free show in Communist polemics that has made Marxist-Leninist ideological quarrels seem to them not only irrelevant but often ridiculous, and indeed a threat to concentration of all anticolonial forces.

Finally, due to the political and economic exigencies facing the Soviets and the Chinese alike, Western (and particularly American, British, and French) policies and actions will probably continue to have significant influence in Africa—most notably in moments of crisis, during which they also influence African attitudes toward the Soviets and the Chinese. The extent of Sino-Soviet influence remains a function not of the appeal of Marxism-Leninism or of the size and effectiveness of Communist parties. Rather, it depends on the succcess of Soviet and Chinese state power in infiltrating, buying, and supplying military aid to the radical racist nationalists of black Africa as opposed to the success of reluctant Western counteraction. But, above all, it remains in the end a function of African affairs themselves: their confusion, instability, and intractability to all foreign attempts at control.

6. Sino-Soviet Rivalry and Southern Africa

—GEORGE A. MARTELLI
—RICHARD V. ALLEN

Since the summer of 1964 the Communist powers have suffered a series of setbacks in Africa and have little to show by way of compensation. From a military point of view the most outstanding of these reverses has been the suppression of insurrection in Angola and Portuguese Guinea and the defeat of the Congolese rebels. Political reverses have included the split in the Organization of African Unity (OAU) and the formation of the Organisation Commune Afrique et Malgache (OCAM);[1] the fall of Ben Bella and the decline in influence of President Nasser—both of whom, as champions of revolutionary nationalism, either willingly or unwittingly served the Communist cause.

The rash of military coups d'état in 1965-66, coupled with the expulsion of Soviet and Chinese political, military, and economic missions from several countries, has served to blunt the Communist penetration of Africa and has caused both Communist and African leaders to reevaluate the future course of events in the continent.

---

[1]The OCAM comprises a group of "moderate" French-speaking states in opposition to the more extreme policies of the OAU.

The Erosion of Influence

All these events, and particularly the failure of the various "liberation" movements to make headway anywhere, have had a dampening effect on revolution and have encouraged the more moderate African leaders (which includes nearly all those in power) to come out openly against the Communists and their African allies and to unite in defense of the status quo. When Chou En-lai stressed the "ripeness" of conditions for revolution in Africa in 1965, Mr. Kenyatta promptly replied that he did not know to which countries the Chinese Premier was referring, but that there would certainly be no revolution in Kenya.

Other African leaders, notably President Houphouet-Boigny of the Ivory Coast, have denounced communism as a greater danger to Africa than colonialism. It was fear of the former, as well as distrust of the old Casablanca group, that brought together the former members of the Afro-Malagasy Union (the UAM—known earlier as the Brazzaville group) and resulted in its revival under the new title of OCAM.

Both groups had been dissolved after the formation of the OAU in 1963, for it was argued that in a united Africa there was no room for regional alliances. However, it was soon shown that genuine African unity was an illusion and that the OAU was being used by extreme elements to impose their leadership on the rest. The resentment of the extremists came to a head over the Congo and resulted in a split which has steadily widened and reduced the OAU to impotence. This was revealed most glaringly in the summer of 1965 when OCAM leaders threatened to boycott the OAU "summit" conference in Accra on the grounds that Ghana had been supporting subversion inside OCAM countries.

Some of them also refused invitations to attend the Afro-Asian Conference of Algiers, pointing out that it was a Communist propaganda stunt and therefore a waste of their time. The fact that neither of these conferences, which were planned to provide a platform for extremists, was held at the scheduled date has been another blow—especially to the Chinese, who had planned to use them to attack both the "imperialists" and the Russians.

In short, during the last year in Africa the reaction has almost amounted to a new "wind of change." Revolution is no longer in the air and the voices of the radicals—Nkrumah, Nasser, Touré—who previously dominated every African conference are now strangely stilled.

To some extent this was only to be expected. The nationalist leaders who are now prime ministers or presidents of independent states realize that their first duty is to govern. And there is no more fervent upholder of the law than the poacher turned gamekeeper. Fear of subversion at home makes them hesitate to support it abroad. Malawi's Dr. Hastings Banda, for example, knows that his chief opponent, Chipembere, is on the best of terms with the Mozambique rebels; Dr. Banda will in consequence do nothing to embarrass the Portuguese. Similarly the suspicion that Holden Roberto was in collusion with the Congolese rebels was one reason (the other being that it had become a public danger) why Tshombe cracked down on his movement, cut off his supplies, and closed his training camp—with the result that for all practical purposes the Revolutionary Government of Angola in Exile (GRAE) has ceased to exist. With the ouster of Tshombe in October 1965, speculation grew concerning the possible re-emergence of Roberto, who accompanied Congolese President Joseph Kasavubu to the Accra OAU Summit Conference. The subsequent coup d'état by the Army in November seemed to indicate that General Mobutu, whose announced intention at that time was to rule for five years, would not countenance use of a Congolese sanctuary for revolutionary exile groups operating against the Congo's neighbors.

Warned by such experiences, Mr. Kaunda—while tolerating the presence of political exiles—keeps a strict eye on all of them and will not allow training camps for guerrillas in Zambia. This is not merely for fear of reprisals by Rhodesia or Portugal, which command Zambia's outlets to the sea, but because the existence of militant revolutionary centers, although not aimed at the country which harbors them, is at best a nuisance and at worst a threat to its security. Kaunda's swift impounding (in September 1965) of an arms shipment in transit to Mozambique rebels in Lusaka is evidence of his position in this matter.

Rebel Military Defeats

Another factor influencing the African leaders—and probably the most important—has been the failure of the revolutionaries to achieve any military success. In this respect the defeat they sustained in the Congo, where a few hundred white mercenaries proved more than a match for ten times as many native guerrillas, was undoubtedly a turning point. Until then the majority of African Governments were sitting on the fence, waiting to come down on the winning side. When they saw that it was Tshombe's, they declared for him. Even Dr. Nkrumah, the most implacable of his enemies, temporarily decided to make his peace with the former Congolese Premier. The withdrawal of support for the Congolese rebels by the Arab countries is equally significant.

There has also been a deep disillusionment with the performance of the "liberation" movements in the Portuguese territories. Both in Angola and Guinea the Portuguese were taken by surprise; but once they had recovered from the shock of attack, they were never in serious danger, not only because of their military superiority but also because of the refusal of the African populations to respond to the revolutionary call. This was particularly marked in Portuguese Guinea, where the natives—as in the enclave of Cabinda and in certain sections of Northern Angola—demanded and were given arms to defend themselves against the rebels. In Portuguese Guinea, Angola, and to a large extent in Mozambique, the uprisings have been limited to one of many tribes; the rest remained loyal, if only for the reason that they knew they would be the first victims were the revolution to succeed.

Those living near frontier areas have had a taste of what this would mean from the behavior of the guerrillas in their villages, where the practice is to recruit by intimidation and to live by extortion. In consequence the arrival of Portuguese troops is usually greeted with relief, and once they have shown they are able to protect the population they rapidly gather the majority on their side.

The absence among Africans of a sense of nationhood is, of course, the biggest handicap of the nationalists and is reflected by the divisions among their leaders, largely tribal in origin. We hear about the quarrels between the two Angolan parties, the Popular Movement for Liberation of Angola (MPLA) and the Union of Angolan Peoples (UPA). But there is equally bitter rivalry in Portuguese Guinea between the African Party for the Independence of Guinea and Cape Verde (PAIGC) and the Front for the Liberation of Independent National Guinea (FLING). And in Mozambique a new organization, the Revolutionary Committee of Mozambique (COREMO), has recently been formed in opposition to the Front for Liberation of Mozambique (FRELIMO), the group headed by Eduardo Mondlane, whom the new party has accused of killing more Africans than Portuguese.

These quarrels have discouraged other African countries from continuing their support. When the African Liberation Committee (Committee of Nine) was set up by the OAU in 1963, it was agreed that each member state should contribute money to the committee in proportion to its national income. Knowing the difficulty of collecting funds for extensive prior commitments, few member states pay their subscriptions regularly. With so many more pressing claims on their impoverished treasuries it would be surprising if there were much enthusiasm for subsidizing revolutions which can bring no benefit to themselves and which in some cases—for instance Malawi, Zambia, and the Congo—could indeed be harmful to their own vital interests.

Certainly the ALC, which has its offices in Dar-es-Salaam, is not a very impressive organization; and there is reason to believe that the various "liberation" movements rely less upon it than upon the aid they receive directly from various countries. Dr. Mondlane, for example, has admitted that he receives "money from the West and arms from the East"; and there is no doubt that the MPLA, which is not recognized by the African governments, is kept going not by the ALC but by the embassies of the Communist countries in Brazzaville, its headquarters.

African leaders will, of course, continue to pay lip service to the nationalist ideal, to denounce the "imperialists," and to agitate at the United Nations for action against the white redoubt. It is doubtful that their actions can extend much farther. They have neither the money, nor the arms, nor the men, to give effective aid to the "liberation" movements. Nor, to tell the truth, have they the will. What, in the final analysis, has any of them to gain by the expulsion, say, of the Portuguese from Angola and Mozambique or the white Rhodesians from Rhodesia? Would it solve any of their own problems or render them any less vulnerable to their radical opposition? The elimination of colonialism is only the first of Communist objectives in Africa; the second is the revolution which would sweep away the pro-Western "bourgeois" regimes left behind by the departing colonialists. Hence for Messrs. Mobutu, Kaunda, and Banda (to mention only those most immediately affected) one guarantee of survival is the presence on their flanks of efficient European armies, which they know will never attack them or allow them to be attacked across the frontiers they control.

It follows that the "liberation" movements will have to rely less and less on the African countries and more and more on the Communists. In addition, they will undoubtedly continue to receive moral and financial support from the West, including Britain and America: for example, children of the Mozambiquan rebels are being educated at a school in Mozambique built by the Ford Foundation and supplied with books by the British Council.

Sino-Soviet Strategies for Africa

The impact on Africa of the Sino-Soviet dispute must be viewed against the background of (1) a widespread reaction among African leaders (or what Premier Tshombe once called the "triumph of realism"); (2) the military defeats sustained by the revolutionaries in the Congo, Angola, Mozambique, and Portuguese Guinea; (3) African disillusionment with the "liberation" movements, inability to assist them except with speeches and resolutions, and limited interest in their success.

The first conclusion which suggests itself is that with or without the dispute the Soviet Union had to react to the entry of China on the African scene or lose the leadership of the revolutionary movement. Otherwise she might have been inclined to draw in her horns after her experiences in Guinea and the Congo where she had backed the wrong contender (Lumumba) and seen her embassy, and those of her satellites, expelled from Leopoldville. As it was, both the Soviet and the East European Communists continued to support the rebellions in the Congo and the Portuguese territories by providing training for the rebels, and by supplying arms through Algeria, Egypt, Congo (Brazzaville), and Zanzibar.

For China, on the other hand, the dispute has undoubtedly provided an additional motive for extending her African activities. Seeing the Soviet Union no longer as an ally in the world struggle to establish communism, but as a liability in any war against "imperialism," it became as important to her to counter Soviet influence in Africa as to oppose that of America or Western Europe. Coming fresher to the battle, China has expended substantial effort to deepen her influence with the young African states. But these efforts have been offset by the combination of incessant threats and apparent espousal of violence as the prime mover of all revolutionary activity. Tempered by the experience and the realities of political, social, and economic administration, the more moderate African leaders have put a quite different construction on the word *revolution*.

Nonetheless, the fact that responsible African leaders have developed both fear and distrust of Chinese strategy for Africa does not grant them automatic immunity to it. Peking has developed important footholds in East Africa (Tanzania, and particularly on the island of Zanzibar) and West Africa (Brazzaville) and shows no signs of willingness to relinquish them. On the contrary, China will seek every opportunity to expand her bases of operations against unstable neighboring regimes and, in some cases, may even be willing to take dangerous and "adventuristic" risks. That the Chinese will follow this course of action is underscored by Lin Piao's speech of September 2, 1965, which graphically describes the mainspring of Chinese revolutionary strategy as one of encircling the city from the countryside.[2] The strategy is one of classical guerrilla warfare—but guerrilla warfare of global proportions, in which Africa is to serve as a crucial testing ground.

The Soviets, who prefer to assist the world revolutionary movement by more subtle and "civilized" means, insist that the "principal contradiction of the epoch" is that between the system of socialism and the system of capitalism. In the long run, the Soviets say, victory will be achieved not by the military encirclement of "capitalism" by openly hostile revolutionary forces which might provoke the former to react

[2]The excerpt from that speech which summarizes Chinese revolutionary strategy appears on page 25.

violently, but by the steady erosion of Western influence, support, and strength. The combination of this weakening process and the vastly increased economic and military power of the "socialist camp" (including, it should be noted, Communist China) will then bring about the desired isolation of the West—principally the United States —and will make the "final stage" of the revolution relatively painless. Above all, the Soviets want to avoid direct Soviet–U.S. confrontation, which they fear may result in uncontrolled escalation and unacceptable damage to the Soviet Union in particular and the "socialist camp" in general.

While this caution and restraint on the part of the Soviets is certainly a function of the lesson learned in the Cuban missile crisis of October 1962, it is by no means a blind fear of the West. Operating on the assumption that time is working on the side of the worldwide revolutionary movement and against the "moribund system of capitalism," Moscow sees no advantage in losing the accumulated benefits of the détente begun in 1963. In support of their approach they point to the deepening crisis within the Western alliance system, the breakdown of trade barriers which give access to Western technology and credits, the increasing "isolation" of the United States and its allies in the United Nations, and the enhanced prestige of the Soviet Union in the entire *tiers monde*.

Thus, as earlier chapters of this volume have pointed out, the essence of the Sino-Soviet split concerns tactics and not strategy, or, as some would have it, means and not ends. Communist China, operating in the underdeveloped world with a degree of reckless abandon while remaining under the protection of the strategic umbrella of the socialist camp, insists that the West is one big "paper tiger." According to the Chinese, the West can readily be either frightened or fought into submission only by a relentless, militant line, particularly in Africa, Asia, and Latin America. The Soviet Union, and along with it the overwhelming majority of the world's Communist parties, argues that the overall balance of power will be tipped in its favor through the successful manipulation of the "correlation of forces," of which the African countries are an important component. This shift in the balance, say the Soviets, must come slowly and cautiously through a prolonged détente; unnecessary provocations and confrontations in even the most remote areas of the world may cause the "paper tiger" to bare his "nuclear teeth."

Both strategies—one "hard-line," the other "soft-line"—make formidable demands on the West, if only in the sense that Sino-Soviet rivalry to implement each requires a wider spectrum of Western response. The announced goals of the United States in Africa, which boil down to the creation of independent, peaceful, and viable national states, will by no means be brought closer to realization if the Sino-Soviet dispute continues at its present pitch. It is not a source of genuine comfort that one party to the split seeks to make the African countries active and militarily offensive stepping stones in the overall struggle against the West, while the other seeks to make them politically offensive participants in a coalition of disparate forces to be directed against the same target.

Mixed Results of Competition

On the other hand, competition between the two countries both assists and damages the revolutionary cause in Africa. It is of assistance because it enlarges the sources of support to rebel movements operating against any established government, black or white. A rebel leader who fails to secure assistance in Moscow can always proceed to Peking and even to Pankow, Prague, or Belgrade—all of whose African operations have been steadily expanding. Even though rebel leaders may be favorably disposed to one or the other strategy, ideological differences leave them unimpressed; and they have shown their willingness to accept money and other help wherever they can find it. Sensing the critical importance of their individual situations to both Moscow and Peking, rebel leaders have become more sophisticated in their bargaining techniques, using the promise of support from one side as a lever to up the ante from the other. Then, too, for a self-respecting revolutionary to be invited to both capitals is almost *de rigueur:* a necessary status symbol.

But Sino-Soviet rivalry is also a cause of disunity. For example, when the Committee of National Liberation was set up by the Lumumbist exiles in Brazzaville to wage war against the Congolese Government of Cyril Adoula, it split almost immediately into a pro-Russian and pro-Chinese wing, each of which was reputed to be accepting advice and money from the respective embassies in Brazzaville. This breach was never healed and contributed to the final disintegration of the rebel leadership after its defeat in the field. Similar differences, arising from the same cause, have been reported in the leadership of the MPLA, which also has its headquarters in Brazzaville.

During the last war the American and British Governments were seldom able to coordinate their support of the various resistance movements in Europe. It would be surprising if the Communists, who dislike and distrust each other much more than the Allies ever did, were any more successful in this respect. Thus the Chinese presence in Africa, while strengthening the revolutionary forces materially, also weakens them morally by creating yet another division in a leadership already split pro- and anti-Western.

The Southern Redoubt

In the last resort the future of the southern half of Africa will depend upon the determination of the "white redoubt" to defend itself. At present this determination shows no sign of flagging. Because of inferior fighting skills, inadequate military leadership, and absence of any articulate nationalist sentiment among the Africans, the guerrilla tactics employed in portions of the redoubt can never be decisive—and their value to the Communists is almost purely political.

Both the Soviet Union and China have a common interest in creating difficult situations for the West at the United Nations and in other international groupings; for this purpose the "liberation" movements, which keep international attention centered on the redoubt, are essential. But if either China or the Soviet Union really wished to achieve any meaningful result against the redoubt, she would need to put an army in Africa. That is scarcely practicable even in disguised form because it would almost certainly bring a swift reaction from the West. An alternative which might serve Sino-Soviet purposes just as well—namely armed intervention by the United Nations—is equally impracticable since it would lead to full-scale war. Rhodesia's Unilateral Declaration of Independence of November 1965 raised this very issue, and it seems unlikely that the route of armed intervention will be chosen to throttle the "illegal regime" of Ian Smith. Reaction to UDI by African leaders was violent, but it was noted that the intensity of the threats leveled by them varied in direct proportion to their distance from Salisbury. Both the Soviets and the Chinese unleashed propaganda barrages at Rhodesia, but neither delivered a sustained attack designed to gather political or military momentum. It was a reflection of the basic attitude shared by the Soviets and Chinese alike that the new state of affairs made very little difference to them; the issue remained the same, i.e., the elimination of the white presence in Africa, whether it be of the British colonial or Rhodesian independent variety.[3]

It is probable, therefore, that while continuing to exploit the issue of anti-colonialism and trying to instill new vigor into the "national liberation movement," the tactics of both Communist powers will be to probe for the softest spot. This must take them away from the southern redoubt, which presents the most formidable obstacle, and toward countries where incompetent administration, regional or tribal quarrels, or economic depression are creating those "excellent conditions for revolution" to which Chou En-Lai was undoubtedly referring in his famous speech. Should that occur, the quarrel between the two Communist powers will matter less than the anarchy which they can jointly or separately create wherever Western influence, symbolized by the European presence, is sufficiently weakened.

---

[3]"The Rhodesian racists would not have dared to carry out their criminal plans without the connivance of the colonialists, who, during recent years, gave the Salisbury racist regime their wholehearted support and strengthened it economically and militarily. . . . Ruling circles in Britain will never be able to escape responsibility for this crime against the African peoples." *Pravda,* November 16, 1965.

See also UN speech of N. T. Fedorenko in *New Times* (Moscow), No. 50, December 15, 1965, pp. 9-12.

The Chinese reaction was similar:

"The declaration of 'independence' by the South Rhodesian White settlers' regime had the connivance and backing of British imperialism. Following that act, British imperialism has continued to play its double-dealing tactics in an attempt to consolidate and stabilize the fascist rule of the racist Smith regime. . . . British imperialism is so keen on shielding and buttressing up the racist regime in Southern Rhodesia not only because it wants to suppress the four million Zimbabwe people's fight for national independence, but also because it intends to make Southern Rhodesia a bridgehead—like South Africa—for the Colonialists and neo-colonialists to commit aggression and encroach upon other regions in Southeast Africa." *Renmin Ribao* editorial, December 18, 1965.

Latin America

7. Background on Communism in Latin America

—*ROBERT J. ALEXANDER*

The Sino-Soviet split has affected both the orthodox Communist parties of Latin America and the groups outside these parties, which are frequently called the "Jacobin left." The situation in Latin America has also been complicated by the phenomenon of the Castro revolution, which combines elements of both orthodox communism and the Jacobin left.

The Orthodox Communists

The orthodox Communists are those parties that either belonged to the Communist International or would belong if it still existed. Such parties are found in every one of the Latin American republics.

Traditionally, the orthodox Communist parties have had two functions. The first was to serve the interests of the Soviet Union. In the early years—before about 1935—the various Latin American parties were quite frank about "the defense of the Soviet Union" being their basic task. Since that time their basic mission has not changed, but they have not been so bold about proclaiming it.

The second function of the Communist parties has been to gain power within the country in which they are operating, for the purpose of establishing a dictatorship and bringing about the social and economic transformations called for by their creed. Before 1959 they had not been very successful in achieving this objective: Communists had served in only three Latin American governments—those of Velasco Ibarra in 1944, Gonzalez Videla in Chile in 1946-47, and Batista in 1942-44. Only in Guatemala under the administration of President Jacobo Arbenz in 1952-54 had they come really near to seizing complete control of a Latin American government.

The Jacobin Left

The Jacobin left consists of small groups and parties in various of the Latin American countries. In some nations there are competing groups of this type. In being xenophobically nationalistic, they are like the French Revolutionary Jacobins—favoring violent social change at any cost and either disparaging political democracy or violently opposing it. Since the advent of the Castro regime, these people have generally come to regard themselves as Marxist-Leninists. However, their relations with the orthodox Communists have not always been the smoothest.

Choosing Sides

The orthodox Communists and the Jacobin leftists have reacted differently to the Sino-Soviet split. The Jacobin left has naturally tended to side with the Chinese; whereas the first reaction of the leadership of the Communist parties was to support the Russians. However to a greater or lesser degree both Communists and Jacobin leftists have been split by the Sino-Soviet problem.

The sympathy of the Jacobin leftists for the Chinese arises from several factors. First of all, the leadership and membership of these groups tend to be very young. They have the rashness of youth and the willingness to undertake venturesome and irresponsible activities—the kind of activities the Chinese encourage. Also, they have no traditional ties to the Soviet Union, and siding with its opponents represents no betrayal of their past. Finally, because they are small groups with no past history of consequence and no present influence among the masses of the people, the Jacobin leftists are willing to engage in the kind of guerrilla activities and urban terrorism which the Chinese advocate.

In contrast, the Communist leaders tend by nature to side with the Soviet Union. The leadership of these parties tends to be middle-aged or older—not the kind of people who will take to the hills with enthusiasm. Furthermore, virtually all of the middle-ranking and higher-level Communist Party leaders have been trained in the Soviet Union. Particularly the top-ranking ones have throughout their adult lives regarded the USSR as the epitome of the kind of society they are trying to establish in their own countries.

The Communist parties have something to lose by launching guerrilla activities and urban terror campaigns. They remain legal in several of the countries, and in some countries they have representation in legislative bodies. They have some degree of influence in the national labor movements; and, in a number of places, they have sizable amounts of property which could be confiscated. In some countries, too, Communist leaders of working-class origin look disparagingly on the young men of upper- and middle-class background who lead the Jacobin left, regarding them as dilettantes in their advocacy of guerrilla activities. Thus in most countries of Latin America, the Communist Party leaders have thrown their support behind the more cautious kind of Latin American policy advocated by the Russians.

Nonetheless, this comparatively moderate position of the Communist leadership has been challenged from within the party ranks. Younger elements, particularly among the students, have been greatly influenced by the Chinese approach. In part this is the conflict of generations that occurs in almost any party. In part, too, it reflects the fact that the young people have not had the training their elders received in Russia; in contrast, many of the young people have been trained in Cuba.

These factors have led to splits in the Communist parties of several countries and there are indications of future divisions in several others.

The Resulting Rifts

The first open split along Sino-Soviet lines took place in Brazil in 1961. A group of leaders, headed by Mauricio Grebols, João Amazones, and Pedro Pomer formed a separate party; it took the name Partido Comunista do Brasil, whereas the party they abandoned assumed the name Partido Comunista Brasileiro. The Prestes party remained the majority group and worked closely with the regime of President João Goulart.

There is no doubt that the overthrow of Goulart represented a severe defeat for the pro-Soviet Communists, whose policy was to infiltrate the Goulart regime rather than to resort to guerrilla warfare. There were indications that a further split in the Prestes party took place as a result of the overthrow of the regime of Goulart in March 1964. The Rio newspaper *O Jornal* reported in October 1964 that Luiz Carlos Prestes had been removed as secretary general of his party by pro-Chinese elements within his own central committee. Subsequently there were unconfirmed rumors that the ousting of Prestes brought a complete schism to the party.

The second split in a Latin American Communist party took place in Ecuador, and the circumstances were rather peculiar. Before the military coup d'état of July 1963, a pro-Chinese group had appeared and challenged the leadership of the pro-Soviet elements controlling the party. The pro-Chinese announced that there would soon be a military coup against the regime of President Carlos Arosemans, who enjoyed Communist support. But the party leaders rejected this thesis. As a result, when the coup actually came the pro-Chinese elements were already in hiding; the pro-Soviet leaders of the party were not and were rounded up by the new military regime.

The Peruvian Communists have also suffered a split. In February

1964 a pro-Chinese group forcibly seized the headquarters of the Communist Party and proclaimed that the leaders of the party were expelled. They then established their own authorities for the party. The pro-Soviet elements fought back, and reorganized their own forces. They continued to control the segment of the labor movement under Communist influence. However, the pro-Chinese element was very strong among the country's students; and in a congress of the Peruvian Students Federation, a coalition of supporters of President Belcúnde, the Aprista Party, and the pro-Soviet Communists was necessary to defeat the candidates of the pro-Chinese group.

There have been minuscule splits in the Chilean and Mexican Communist Parties. However, there were indications that the Chilean Party was going through a profound crisis as a result of the defeat of its nominee for President in the September 1964 election. The Chilean Party had been one of the most outspokenly pro-Soviet parties in Latin America and had squarely denounced both the Chinese Communists' and Fidel Castro's meddling in the internal affairs of the Chilean Party. They strongly supported the idea that it is possible for a pro-Communist regime to come to power through constitutional processes and regarded any suggestion to launch guerrilla war in Chile as quixotic.

The September 1964 election, which put Christian Democratic nominee Eduardo Frei in the Presidency, represented a major defeat for the pro-Soviet position. There was, therefore, a good deal of discontent in the rank and file of the Communist Party; several of the important regional groups of the party were taken over by pro-Chinese elements opposed to the present leadership of the party. The further defeat of the Communists in the March 1965 congressional elections intensified the pressure on the pro-Soviet leadership of the Chilean Communist Party.

The Venezuelan Communist Party presents a special case, for it is the one Communist group in Latin America which put into practice the kind of program for seizure of power that the Chinese advocate. Yet they managed to keep the support not only of the Chinese party but that of the Soviet Union as well. Nevertheless, there is considerable indication that the Venezuelan party is torn by internal conflict.

Since early 1962 the Communist Party of Venezuela (PCV) and

the Movimiento de Izquierda Revolucionaria (MIR) have supported campaigns of guerrilla war in the countryside and terrorism in the cities. At its April 1964 central committee meeting, the Communist Party resolved to continue the guerrilla war, in spite of the fact that violence had not prevented the people from voting in the December 1963 poll.

However this problem has caused serious controversy within the party since at least early 1963. Attempts by some of the older leaders of the party to get a national conference to call off the violence campaign were thwarted by younger elements. Since the 1963 election some of the leaders of both the PCV and the MIR have been urging a return to constitutional activities.

The situation in Cuba is of particular significance in Latin America insofar as the Sino-Soviet split is concerned.

The Cuban United Party of the Socialist Revolution (PURSC), which was formed by a merger of Castro's followers and the old-line Communist Party, was one of the nineteen Communist parties—including the Argentine and Brazilian parties—called together by the CPSU in Moscow in March 1965. But Castro at the same time kept open his lines of communication with the Chinese.

Other things being equal, Fidel Castro is the logical leader of the pro-Chinese Communists in the hemisphere. He, after all, has successfully carried out the kind of revolution the Chinese advocate. Furthermore, the Cuban leaders seem to be convinced that their own regime will not be safe until there is a similar revolution somewhere on the Latin American continent. Unfortunately for Castro, however, other things are not equal. Castro cannot afford to be abandoned by the Russians, who are contributing perhaps a million dollars a day to the Cuban economy.

There is little doubt that Castro is caught in a bind as a result of the Sino-Soviet dispute. He has frequently issued pleas for peace between the two sides—something he undoubtedly devoutly desires. Within Latin America, however, there is little doubt that Castro aspires to be the leader of the Latin American Communist revolution. He has been giving various kinds of support to Chinese-type movements against Latin American regimes; he and his associates have also been critical of the Communist elements who have been more prone to follow a peaceful road to power. Ernesto Guevara was particularly outspoken in such criticism.

Yet there has not been any open break between the Cuban leadership and the more pro-Soviet Communist parties in Latin America. Representatives of the official Communist parties of Latin America who met in Havana in 1964 came out in strong support of the Cuban revolution.

The full impact of the Sino-Soviet split is not likely to be felt in Latin America until either the Chinese or Soviet Party forces the issue to a point where each national Communist party must take a stand and declare its alignment. At that point the Chinese will try to unite their supporters from within the old line with the Jacobin leftists to form single, disciplined parties which can be part of the worldwide Communist movement led by the Chinese. At the same time, the Russians will undoubtedly try to consolidate those groups that remain loyal to them. Equivocation on this issue will then become a luxury which none of the Latin American parties can any longer afford.

Some Accounts of Latin American Splits

Information on the impact of the Sino-Soviet split on the Latin American Communist parties is scattered. However, the following material, gathered largely from Communist sources and personal correspondence with well-informed Latin Americans, gives some indication of the nature of the impact.

An informal count of the Communist parties of Latin America took place at the East German Party Congress in January 1963. Orlando Millas, of the Chilean Politburo, spoke for those Latin American parties that sided with the Soviets against "the provocations of the Albanian leaders." He spoke not only for his party, but also for those of Argentina, Bolivia, Brazil, Colombia, Costa Rica, Ecuador, Guatemala, Haiti, Honduras, Nicaragua, Panama, Paraguay, Peru, the Dominican Republic, El Salvador, and Uruguay. The Venezuelans did not sign this.

Argentina

The Communist Party of Argentina is almost completely pro-Soviet. In July 1964, in connection with the calling of the Moscow Conference of Communist Parties, it expressed its solidarity with Moscow in the following terms:

> The leaders of the Chinese Communist Party, who pose as the only defenders of the colonial and dependent countries, propose to exclude from the preparatory organization commission of an international Communist conference, the Communist Parties of Brazil and Argentina, which took an active part in the preparations for the conference of 1960. They are trying in this way to leave Latin America without any representation in this commission.

Bolivia

The Bolivian Communist Party's position has been in support of the Soviet party, although the PCB has had to expel a number of leaders who were pro-Chinese in their orientation. The Trotskyite Partido Obrero Revolucionario was reported to be more pro-Chinese than the Partido Communista de Bolivia.

Brazil

There are at least two Communist parties in Brazil; the split took place in 1961. Ex-Communist writer Osvaldo Peralva described the split in the following terms:

> The Amazonas-Grabois-Pomar group, after dominating important fractions of the party in Rio Grande do Sul, the State of Rio and São Paulo, broke with the party dominated by Prestes (which had decided to call itself Partido Comunista Brasileiro, instead of Partido Comunista do Brazil) and declared itself heir of the latter; that is, of the Partido Comunista do Brasil, and adopted that name. It established its own leadership apart, founded a publishing house, Edicoes Futuro Ltda, which brought out the

book of Ché Guevara, *Guerrilla War,* and announced other books, written by Amazonas, Pomar, Grabois, Kalil Chede, Lincoln Oest, and other elements expelled from the party of Prestes, according to announcements in *Novos Rumos*. The most significant fact is that among the volumes announced was one with the title *Living Marxism Through Its Masters,* a collection of works of Marx, Engels, Plekhanov, Lenin, Stalin, and Mao Tse-tung. The defiance was clear: Stalin and Mao Tse-tung among the masters of Marxism.

The reaction of the two parties to the overthrow of Goulart was different. The Prestes party called for the Communists to put themselves "in the advance guard of the workers in strikes, in the advance guard of the peasants in the struggle for agrarian reform, and in the advance guard of the Brazilian people which is engaged in resistance."

In contrast, the pro-Chinese party insisted that the fall of Goulart had demonstrated that the pacific road to revolution had failed, that cooperation with the national bourgeoisie around Goulart had been unsuccessful, and that only violent revolution remained.

However, it was also reported that some from the pro-Soviet party had crossed over to the idea of violent upheaval and that some militants of the party had gone to Cuba for training. One of these was the leader Luiz Barreira Araujo. At the same time, Lionel Brizola had with open arms accepted the Prestes party as collaborators. (Brizola is a brother-in-law of ex-President João Goulart and a former Governor of Rio Grande do Sul.)

The pro-Russian party may have undergone a further split after the fall of Goulart. An article in *O Jornal* of Rio de Janeiro on October 20, 1964, read as follows:

> Sr. Luiz Carlos Prestes was deposed 15 days ago from his post of secretary general of the Communist Party, after a meeting of the central committee of the party, his deposition being interpreted by sources allied with communism "as a consequence of discord between the policy of Red China and the line dictated by the Russian C.P."
>
> Today comes the news that the substitute for Prestes will be Mario Alves, although he is in jail and doesn't appear in the report of the junta established to run the organization; and the definitive choice of someone to succeed Prestes must be made soon.

Chile

The Chilean Communist Party has been strongly on the side of the Russians and has carried on a public polemic with the Chinese Communist Party. Characteristic of the polemic was the following statement by Luis Corvalan, secretary general of the party, in June 1963:

> If the Communist Party of China considers our position to be erroneous, it could address itself to the central committee of our party, officially presenting to us its point of view or inviting us to a bilateral conversation. This would be the proper procedure. But what has happened is that, disregarding all the norms fixed for interparty relations, it has devoted itself, as has been said, to propagating its erroneous concepts in the ranks of our party, to attempting to influence our members, to winning supporters for its line. This is without a doubt an unfriendly attitude, an undermining, splitting, and disruptive activity.
>
> The matter becomes even graver if one takes into account that in order to do this it has sought the collaboration of party members, recruited individually and against the will of our central committee, which has been expressly made known to the Chinese comrades. The attitude of the Communist Party of China does not conform to its repeated declarations regarding the equality of all the parties.

The Chilean Communists have also quarreled with Castro and other Cuban leaders. Luis Corvalan published an article in January 1963 which said in part:

> The fact that in Cuba the revolution came to power by the violent road is sometimes interpreted as signifying that this is the only road for all the countries of the continent. But the contribution consists, firstly, in having demonstrated the possibility of breaking with imperialism in Latin America; secondly, in having demonstrated the possibility of taking the road of the construction of socialism; and thirdly, in having demonstrated that the triumph of a people's national liberation, and further on, socialist revolution is not necessarily bound up with an international war.

> As for the manner of making the revolution, history has vindicated Fidel Castro. Even more, one may safely assume that the road taken over there is also, speaking in general terms, the most probable road in other countries, perhaps in most of the countries of the continent. But there can be no certainty that all of them will take this road. Such a certainty would lead to the abandonment of positions already conquered and to the neglect of factual potentialities.
>
> At this stage of the development of events in Chile it may be affirmed that objectively the revolutionary process is taking a peaceful road which, in accordance with reality, our party pointed out. In practice, all the parties of the Popular Action Front agree on this point. The adventurers and dogmatists have been pushed aside.

Late in 1963 a group of intellectuals—the Sparticists—was expelled from the Chilean Communist Party; early in 1964 it formed a new party of little significance. However, the *Peking Review* wrote up the January 1964 meeting of expelled Communists in the May 1, 1964, issue and noted its pro-Chinese statements.

Colombia

The Colombian Communist Party has made clear its support of the Russians. A meeting of the central committee at the end of June 1964 affirmed its solidarity with the Soviet position, condemned again the schismatic activities of the Chinese, and called for a world Communist conference. This resolution was broadcast by TASS.

As early as 1963, however, the Colombian Communist Party in a plenum of the central committee suggested a dual policy for Colombia—at once democratic and violent. It was decided to form "self-defense units" led by the party. In June 1964 a plenum of the central committee endorsed the armed struggle of peasants in the Marquetelia region. Shortly afterward *Voz Proletaria,* the Communist periodical, proclaimed: "Guerrilla war is invincible. Guerrilla war such as exists in our country especially among the peasants of Marquetelia, or as is followed by the people of Vietnam, is invincible in spite of all of the enormous military force which is brought to bear against it."

Among the Communist youth there has been trouble with pro-Chinese elements. In the Fifth Plenum of the Central Committee of the YCL in February 1964, there was a demand that the party pass from self-defense to offense. This was approved; but when it was also agreed to participate in elections, a minority of the YCL Central Committee withdrew. The leader of the dissidents was Sergio de la Torre, who had been expelled from the Soviet Union. The pro-Chinese in May 1964 established a periodical, *Estudios de la Juventud.*

In 1963 the Communist Party was engaged in a polemic with the Movimiento de Obreros, Estudiantes y Campesinos, a Castroite group.

Cuba

In *La Guerra de Guerrillas,* Ernesto Guevara noted that "it is not necessary to wait until all conditions for making revolution exist; the insurrection can create them"; he denounced "the defeatist attitude of revolutionaries or pseudo-revolutionaries who remain inactive and take refuge in the pretext that against a professional army nothing can be done, and who sit down to wait until in some mechanical way all necessary objective and subjective conditions are given without working to accelerate them."

He also attacked "those who maintain dogmatically that the struggle of the masses is centered in city movements, entirely forgetting the immense participation of the country people in the life of all the underdeveloped parts of America."

Ecuador

On March 31, 1964, the central committee of the pro-Russian Communist Party issued a statement saying:

> All of the force and means of the factionalists and splitters, of the partisans of the "Chinese revolutionary line" has been devoted since the establishment of the dictatorship in Ecuador, to attacking the party, calumniating its leaders, who have sought refuge in hiding to continue the struggle, attempting to destroy the direction of the party. They have thus aided the military dictatorship to

> fight against the party. . . . The Ecuadorian Communist Party affirms that all those who have isolated themselves from the general lines of the world Communist movement, all who have sought to decapitate the directing organs of the party, all who have attempted schism, have had the direct support of the Chinese leaders.

Panama

The Partido del Pueblo de Panama, the Communist Party of that republic, attacked advocates of armed insurrection in November 1962:

> Leftist deviationism is another form in which petty-bourgeois opportunism manifests itself. This deviation, which at present is the most active, impedes the development of the mass struggle and induces the masses quietly and fatalistically to wait for the appearance of men of destiny. This leftist current postulates that revolution in Panama should take the form of insurrection, but understanding by this only one of its forms, namely guerrilla warfare. Starting from a subjective analysis which disregards the real development of events in our country and overestimating the revolutionary capacity of the masses, they claim that all the conditions for such a form of struggle are already fulfilled. Nevertheless, they do nothing to convince the people of the necessity to take up the struggle for the solution of its problems. The leftist deviationists maintain a mistaken position in regard to the movement of the masses and in regard to the party, in regard to the Communists even though they claim to be Marxists-Leninists.

Paraguay

The Paraguayan Party has been split into two factions—the pro-Peking group apparently led by Oscar Credyt and the pro-Moscow group by Alfonso Guerra, Alfonso Alcorta, and Obdulio Barthe. In 1964 Barthe issued a strong message of support for the Soviet Party's position on calling an international Communist conference.

Peru

The origins of the split in the Peruvian Communist Party date at least from 1958 when the Lima committee of the party, at its Fifteenth Departmental Congress, denounced the national leadership of the party and called for a new national committee, which it called the Comité Central Provisional Leninista.

The pro-Moscow party was led by Barrio, Acosta, and del Prado; the pro-Peking one, by Saturnino Paredes. The pro-Moscow party papers are *Unidad* and *Jovenguardia;* the pro-Peking papers are *Bandera Roja* and *Peru Juvenil.*

In April 1964, after the issuing of the Suslov report against the Chinese party, Jorge del Prado expressed total support for the Soviet position, while *Bandera Roja* supported the Chinese point of view. At the end of June 1964 the nineteenth plenum of the central committee of the pro-Soviet party expressed support for the world Communist conference being sponsored by Khrushchev, and denounced the "Chinese divisionists."

The pro-Peking party denounced the international Communist meeting called by Khrushchev. In doing so, it commented:

> The Peruvian Communist Party supports and acclaims the firm attitude taken by the great Communist Party of China and by the Korean, Albanian, Japanese, Indonesian, and other Marxist-Leninist parties which are now raising higher than ever the banner of Marxism-Leninism against the corrupt revisionist trend and exposing the schismatic maneuvers of the international clique of Khrushchev and Tito.

The pro-Peking party also celebrated the overthrow of Khrushchev:

> The Political Commission of the Central Committee of the Communist Party of Peru acclaims Khrushchev's removal from office with genuine revolutionary emotions and hopes that the new leaders of the CPSU and the Soviet Government will firmly adhere to Marxism-Leninism and proletarian internationalism. Modern revisionism, which Khrushchev and his supporters intro-

duced into the CPSU, should be uprooted. This is an indispensable condition for the party of Lenin and Stalin to become once again the "shock brigade" of the world Communist and workers' movement.

Uruguay

In January 1964, Jaime Perez, a member of the Politburo of the Communist Party of Uruguay, published an article which said:

> Our party feels that when the principles of Marxism-Leninism are in question, there cannot be any neutrals. From the beginning we, like the Communist Party of the Soviet Union and the whole international Communist movement, have adopted a firm attitude. Neutrality, under the circumstances, can only weaken our movement, because it plays the game of the divisionists.

Rodney Arismendi, Uruguayan Communist leader whom Moscow has often regarded as a general Latin American spokesman, wrote in the October 1964 issue of *World Marxist Review* (the organ of the pro-Moscow parties) as follows:

> Contrary to the arbitrary assertions of the Chinese leaders, we must say that whatever mistakes the Communist parties made they can in no way be attributed to the Twentieth Congress; on the contrary, these mistakes were the result of an inconsistent appraisal of the theses set forth by that congress. On the other hand, it may rightly be said that without the analysis of the fundamental problems of the revolutionary movement made by the Twentieth Congress, and without the affirmation of the spirit of true internationalism, Cuba and with it our own revolution would be exposed to some devastating blows.

In the same article, he commented: "In a word, the victory of the continental revolution directly depends on our ability to find paths of struggle adequate to the actual conditions, and to master all forms of struggle and social actions."

However, pro-Chinese elements were reportedly active in Uruguay. They were said to be behind the establishment in June 1963 of the periodical *Epoca*. It was also reported that Enrique Rodriguez, Communist senator, and Eduardo Viera, editor of *El Popular,* the Communist paper, were pro-Chinese or at least were leaning toward violent revolutionary action. The Socialist Party, led by Vivian Trias, was also reportedly becoming increasingly pro-Chinese; it was certainly violently pro-Castro.

Venezuela

The Venezuelan Communist Party has supported the use of violence since early 1962. A meeting of the party's central committee in April 1964 was reported by Carlos Lopez in the *World Marxist Review* of October 1964 to have "confirmed the general line of our party concerning the use of force in the revolutionary denouement of the Venezuelan situation and armed struggle on the basic form of the development of the revolution." This resolution received the approval of both the pro-Moscow and pro-Peking segments of the international Communist movement, the latter being indicated by an article in the *Peking Review.*

However, there have been recurring reports of divisions within both the Communist Party and the Jacobin-leftist Movimiento de Izquierda Revolucionaria over the Peking-Moscow split and the failure of the Cubans to take a clear position on it. This has been reflected within Venezuela as a split between those who want to return to the use of constitutional instead of violent means.

The situation has been clearer in the MIR than in the PCV. In the former party, Simon Saez Merida was leading the pro-Peking group, while Domingo Alberto Rangel, J. M. Casal, Americo Chacon, and Julio C. Casique were in favor of a return to civic action. In the Communist Party the split has not been so clear, and there appeared to be unity of action.

8. The Role of Cuba

—RICHARD PATTEE

The Cuban revolution has had an undeniable influence on subversion in other parts of Latin America. Initially, during the period when the Communist nature of the 26th of July Movement was not publicly acknowledged, the revolution was hailed as the triumph of resolute men against an entrenched dictatorship with all the means of suppression at its disposal. Fidel Castro emerged as the romantic figure—a gallant David and the legitimate heir of the tradition of José Martí and the insurgents of the last century. There is nothing more illuminating in the technique of revolution than the transformation of this victorious crusade—supported in 1959 by the middle class, the professionals, and a large segment of the peasantry—into the international conspiracy which it is today.

Cuba has assumed the role of symbol for those who seek violent change in Latin America. Perhaps the most fundamental influence is the persistence of the Castro regime for seven years in open defiance of the United States and the formal condemnation of most of the Latin American states. The Cuban government has engaged in aid and encouragement to clandestine guerrilla fighters in Latin America. Castro has made it plain more than once that a primary objective of this effort is Venezuela. The FALN movement in that republic has been able to train many of its members in Cuba and has received arms from Castro.[1]

This is the practical side of Cuban activity. There is also the theoretical aspect—that is, Cuba's contribution to new ideas and a revision of the strategy of revolution. Ernesto Guevara, in his writings and declarations, became something of the recognized authority on how to make one's own revolution. José Manuel Fortuny, writing in the *World Marxist Review* states that:

> The most significant feature of this revolution is that it changed the thinking of the Marxist-Leninist parties and their leaders.[2]

It is not the purpose of this brief survey to trace the course of the Cuban revolution nor to bring out the step by step integration of Cuba into the Soviet-dominated bloc. The intention is to stress the various events of the past year or two which confirm two things: (1) the growing significance of Cuba as the center for subversion and (2) the relation of the Cuban regime to the controversy between the Soviet Union and Red China.

The activist character of the Cuban regime was proclaimed without ambiguity in 1963 by the Special Consultative Committee on Security of the Pan American Union:

> Castroism is nothing more than a collateral movement that obeys extracontinental instructions and directives and is used principally for the purpose of confusing public opinion.[3]

That Fidel Castro is not restricted geographically in the field of subversion and revolution may be gleaned from his speech of October 3, 1965, at the time of the reorganization of the Cuban Communist Party:

> We are striving not only for a communist society but a communist world.[4]

---

[1]James Nelson Goodsell, "Venezuela: No. 1 Subversive Target," *The Christian Science Monitor* (Boston), January 10, 1966. "It was this supplying of the FALN with arms that led to the Organization of American States action in July 1964 which almost cut Cuba adrift from the hemisphere organization."

[2]Toronto, Vol. VIII, No. 8 (August 1965).

[3]Pan American Union (OAS) Ser. L/X/11/4. October 18, 1963, p. 15.

[4]Information Bulletin issued by *World Marxist Review* (Toronto, 1965), p. 25.

Meeting of the Communist Parties, Havana, October 1964

During 1963 and 1964 communism suffered several serious reverses in Latin America, notably in Chile, Brazil, and Venezuela. The Conference of Communist Parties held in Havana in October of 1964 may be interpreted as an exercise in autocriticism and an attempt to evaluate the course of future action. This meeting, which received relatively little publicity, may be taken as a prelude or dress rehearsal, on a hemispheric scale, to the Tri-Continental Conference of January 1966.

Twenty-three Communist parties were represented at the meeting in 1964, including the Soviet Union but not the Peoples Republic of China. This historic gathering was seen as a serious attempt on the part of the Soviet Union to assure absolute control not only of Cuba, who is already dependent on the USSR economically and whose freedom of action is therefore limited, but of the direction of Communist activity throughout Latin America. The Soviets seemed pleased with the results of this increased cooperation:

> There is growing cooperation among the communist parties on a continental scale. This cooperation manifests itself in conferences and meetings of the representatives of communist parties of Central and South America. The conference of the Latin American communist parties at the end of 1964 did much to broaden such contacts.[5]

A French commentator on the same event concluded that: "For a time the USSR has achieved a real success in the struggle being carried on between it and China to attract to its cause the various communist parties in individual countries."[6]

This was a decisive moment in the history of Cuban-Soviet relations. The progress toward total integration of the Caribbean island into the Soviet system had been going on since early 1960 when Khrushchev had declared that the USSR was in full sympathy with the Cuban aspirations for national independence. This was followed by the visit

---

[5]A. Shulgovsky, "Political Trends in Latin America," *International Affairs* [Moscow] (November 1965), p. 49.

[6]Georges Albertini, in *Est et Ouest* (Paris), June 16-30, 1965, pp. 1-6.

of Deputy Premier Anastas Mikoyan to Havana and the signing of a trade pact. By December 19, 1960, the Cubans had concluded a virtual alliance with the Soviet Union. In the joint communiqué issued at that time the two nations agreed to adopt the same position with reference to the principal problems facing the world. Then in May 1961 came the pronouncement of Fidel Castro that Cuba was a "socialist" state—with all the implications of no elections, no popular consultation, and the apparatus of suppression. The great confrontation of October 1962 was the peak in this rapidly evolving situation.

One of the significant consequences of Cuba's relations at this time with the Soviet Union was the abandonment by Castro of the idea of industrialization. He was forced to announce that henceforth the Cuban economy would operate on the basis of the international division of labor—that is, that Cuba would continue to emphasize sugar and other raw materials.

"Thereafter the Cuban leader for a time bowed to the Soviet wish that he mute his strident calls for violent revolution in Latin America and concentrate on domestic economic problems."[7] The Communist Party conclave of 1964 would indicate, therefore, that if there had been a "muting" of the policy of revolutionary activity, it was being abandoned. It is also possible that the alarming growth of terrorist movements in numerous Latin American countries, and the well-known reluctance of some of the orthodox Communist parties in territories affected by these disturbances to engage their responsibility, is a factor that explains this collective consultation of the various national Communist groups.

Reorganization of the Cuban Government

Another event that merits some attention is the reorganization of the Cuban government and its Politburo in the autumn of 1965, prior to the meeting of the Tri-Continental Conference at Havana.

Six of the eight members of the revamped Politburo of the Communist Party are military. Fidel Castro remains as Prime Minister and

[7]Sauripada Bhattacharya, "Cuban-Soviet Relations under Castro, 1959-1964," *Studies on the Soviet Union,* Vol. IV, No. 3 (Munich: New Series, 1965), p. 35.

Secretary General of the Party, and his brother, Major Raúl Castro as Deputy Prime Minister and Minister of the Armed Forces. The two surviving civilians in the combination are Dr. Osvaldo Dorticós Torrado as President and Dr. Armando Hart as Minister of Education and Executive Secretary of the Communist Party.

In the personnel shift it is to be noted that several sectors of the national life are not represented, such as foreign affairs, labor, and economic policy. It may be added that in the new distribution of responsibilities, Major Raúl Castro holds the post of President of the State Security Commission—indicating that there has been a substantial tightening up of both internal security and surveillance and a concentration of effective authority in the hands of a committee overwhelmingly military in makeup.

The Tri-Continental Conference

The first solidarity conference of the representatives of Asia, Africa, and Latin America met in Havana January 3 to 15, 1966. Since the end of the last war the Communist world has certainly created some sort of a record of international conferences, meetings, and summits. One more conference, involving the so-called Third World, does not come as a particular surprise. Nevertheless, the Havana meeting marks a very definite transformation in the evolution of these efforts over the past decade. Afro-Asian solidarity has been brandished as one of the decisive forces in human affairs ever since the memorable Bandung meeting in 1955. The Havana conference represents, however, the expansion of the geography of agitation to include Latin America. To be sure, Latin Americans had attended other meetings as observers, but the Tri-Continental Conference marked the first formal linking of the three continents as part of a unified movement of subversion. A Cuban publication found the meetings significant because:

> Laos, Cambodia, the Congo and Santo Domingo are names that represent different situations which are not necessarily identical, but where the same crimes are being committed with the same fundamental features and which have one single cause: imperialism.[8]

[8] "Tres continentes en marcha," *Cuba* [Havana] (December 1965), p. 23.

The significance of this new grouping is far-reaching. Asia and Africa emerged into independence in most cases after World War II—in the case of Africa in 1960. Although the Afro-Asian group of nations represents something more showy than substantial in terms of unity, there was the common denominator of a recently acquired independence, an affinity in economic and social underdevelopment, and a very real community of sentiment regarding European domination of the past. The elusive nature of these relations both within the United Nations and outside has been amply demonstrated.[9] Anticolonialism could be used with very considerable emotional effect by leaders in territories that had recently experienced European control. Latin America, on the other hand, is five generations away from its attainment of independence. Political independence, at least, has become sufficiently ingrained as to be no longer either a novelty or something which must be constantly proven, precisely because it is not new. Latin America, to a far greater degree than the nations of Africa or Asia, belongs to the West and partakes of its culture and way of life. Aside from certain historical contacts of importance, Latin America has never been closely identified with either Asia or Africa. Now for the first time the three continents have been linked as a common area for violent political and social change. The significance of the Tri-Continental Conference is therefore enormous in terms of the strategy of revolution. It will be a matter of the keenest interest to observe how a common front is to be worked out between such countries as Argentina, Brazil, Uruguay, Chile, and Mexico—with their relatively important middle class—and the totally pre-capitalistic states of Africa.

The second aspect of the Havana conference of fundamental importance was the nature of its composition. Although convoked, as a Soviet commentator reported, by the "anti-imperialist" forces of the three continents, the list of delegates reveals a remarkably high percentage of activists, saboteurs, and terrorists.[10] In a word, the conference was given over primarily to speeches, exhortations, and resolutions by those who are engaged in various parts of the world in the

---

[9]Samaan Boutros Farajallah, *Le groupe afro-asiatique dans le cadre des Nations Unies* (Geneva, 1963).

[10]D. Volsky, "Tri-Continental Conference," *New Times* (Moscow), December 7, 1965.

actual creation of disorder. Only a minimum of attention was devoted to the political and theoretical aspects of world revolution.

The origins of this conference go back to 1961 at the time of the meeting of Latin American revolutionary organizations in Mexico City. The Afro-Asian Solidarity Conference at Moshi in Tanzania gave the then tentative project its blessing, and at Accra in the spring of 1965 definitive approval was accorded the undertaking. The agenda was prepared at Cairo in September of 1965, and the appeal for delegates was sent forth in the name of world peace, solidarity, anti-colonialism, and the eradication of capitalist slavery. Soviet comment prior to the meeting stressed the vital importance of bringing together the Afro-Asian movement and Latin America—indicating that this had not been done in a formal way because of the higher standard of living in the nations of the Western Hemisphere and their greater concern with United States imperialism on their doorstep than with "senile European colonialism."[11] The Chinese showed keen interest in the projected meeting, particularly after the fiasco of the conference that was to have taken place in Algeria.

The role of Cuba was, of course, preeminent at this meeting. Obviously the fact that the conference was held on the only territory in America under Communist dispensation made it particularly significant. In addition to the prestige value for the Castro regime, the Havana congress was a source of encouragement to the groups everywhere in Latin America who have set out on the precarious road of violent subversion.[12]

One of the concrete results was the establishment of a Latin American Solidarity Organization with headquarters in Havana. There has been considerable speculation that many of the delegates, particularly the Egyptian and others from the Afro-Asian world, were reluctant to go along with a permanent secretariat in Havana. Aside from reasons of tradition in this sort of international action, there was the question of the difficulties of transportation to and from Cuba and its remoteness from the main theaters of subversive operations on the other two continents.

---

[11] *Ibid.*

[12] The leftist publication, *Jeune Afrique* (Paris-Tunis), January 30, 1966, p. 18, claims that the conference produced great satisfaction among those "who were most eager for it, the Latin American revolutionary movements."

It was equally plain that, despite the constant insistence on the absolute unity of all liberation movements everywhere and the need for maximum solidarity, the Latin Americans took full advantage to strengthen their own lesser front. The twenty-seven Latin American delegations present met under the presidency of Major Pedro Medina Silva of the Venezuelan National Liberation Front, a fairly clear indication that the initiative was monopolized by the clandestine and terrorist movements. In fact the whole emphasis was placed on the so-called "liberation" movements, ranging from the guerrilla elements in the backwashes of Peru to the Union of Angolan Peoples hanging on precariously in northern Angola.

The sweep of the resolutions and declarations embraces the whole earth. Resolutions specifically called for the intensification of "liberation" movements in Puerto Rico, Martinique, and Guadeloupe as well as in those American republics now under regimes considered reactionary and oppressive. No American republic except Cuba itself was outside the scope of the new program of subversion. This was no conference of delegates "left of center" who condemned the Paraguayan regime or Castelo Branco in Brazil but were reticent about denouncing Mexico which still glories in its socialism. All Latin America was proclaimed the area of operation for those seeking to bring about the revolution.

The principal Soviet delegate, Sharaf Rashidov, took particular pains to express firm solidarity with the fighting people of the Dominican Republic, Southern Rhodesia, South Africa, the Congo, Angola, Puerto Rico [*sic*] and other countries of Asia, Africa, and Latin America. "There is not, nor can there be, any peaceful coexistence between the oppressed peoples and their oppressors."[13]

The resolutions and conclusions of the conference run the entire gamut of politics and geography. Although a great deal of attention was devoted to Vietnam, the items referring to Latin America and therefore within the special competence of the Latin American Solidarity group include the following:

1. Increased solidarity with the peoples of Latin America because they are either struggling with arms in hand against the native oligarchies which serve the United States as in Vene-

[13] "Havana Firm for Solidarity," *Soviet Weekly* (London), February 6, 1966.

zuela, Colombia, Peru, and Guatemala, or are suffering the brutal repression of military tyrants, as in Ecuador, Bolivia, and other countries. Latin America constitutes the rearguard of the most powerful and brutal imperialism, the principal supporter of colonialism and neocolonialism the world over.

2. The Conference calls for maximum militant solidarity with the Latin American peoples, especially the Dominican Republic, whose territory has been overrun and stained with blood by Yankee marines.
3. Puerto Rico remains under the occupation of American imperialism which not only denies its right to independence but has turned it into a huge military base.
4. Solidarity with the Puerto Rican people and demand for the abolition of colonialism in that and other American territories such as the Guianas, Martinique, and Guadeloupe.
5. The transfer of full powers to the puppet government of British Guiana is merely nominal independence serving as a screen for the establishment of an Anglo-American neocolonialist state.
6. Solidarity with Cuba merits special mention. The choice of this country as the seat of the First Conference of Solidarity of the Peoples of Africa, Asia, and Latin America is the highest acknowledgment of its revolution.
7. Nothing can stop the development of the revolutionary struggle in Latin America. Venezuela proves this. . . . the Venezuelan oligarchy has been unable to shake the struggle for liberation.
8. The Panama Canal Zone is being used as a base for the peoples who are fighting for their liberation and with the military base at Guantanamo and the bases at Puerto Rico it makes up the Caribbean triangle.
9. The Indian population of various Latin American countries exists in a similar situation of discrimination of that of the Afro-American population in the United States—the Conference denounces the discriminatory treatment of the Indian population.

The Soviets managed to secure approval for a resolution on peaceful coexistence which was not at all pleasing to the Chinese. This resolution was included, however, as a special item and not incorporated in the general declaration—in a word, a dilution of the proposal. In spite of this apparent moderation on the part of the Soviets, it may be pertinent to quote the commentary of the *Moscow News* which establishes a careful distinction regarding "peaceful coexistence":

> Peaceful coexistence refers exclusively to relations between states having different social and political regimes. . . . the principle of peaceful coexistence cannot be applied the way the imperialists and their lackeys would like to apply it, to restrict the rights of people to social revolution.[14]

Effects of the Conference on Sino-Soviet Estrangement

It is easy to discover ample evidence of the rivalry and the indignation of the Chinese as reflected in broadcasts and press commentaries, particularly with regard to the Soviet insistence on the resolution on peaceful coexistence. The asperity of the Peking reaction may be gleaned from the following excerpts:

> The Khrushchev revisionists tried in vain to impose their capitulationist and divisive line on the conference.
>
> Soviet delegates resorted to all kinds of despicable means to smuggle into the conference their contraband "peaceful coexistence" and all that sort of rubbish.[15]

The interpretations of the significance of the conference have been varied and numerous. Most commentators see in the deliberations an acceleration of revolutionary activism, especially in Latin America, and a serious commitment on the part of the Soviet Union to accommodate to the pace of armed subversion as it seems to be emerging. The tone of the conference would indicate that the Soviet Union, far more experienced in this sort of thing and long associated in international meetings with the governments of other countries, was forced to adjust its declarations and perhaps its future action to the less responsible Chinese who have heretofore had very little contact with the Latin American world. The *Washington Post*

---

[14]February 5, 1966, pp. 14-15.

[15]*Peking News,* January 21, 1966, p. 17.

reported that the meeting was to a "considerable extent a tug of war between the pro-Moscow and the pro-Peking factions of the international Communist movement."[16]

Although the large Soviet delegation (34) and the still larger Chinese (43) disputed any number of procedural and ideological matters, both joined in the support of the resolutions and the statement of the objectives of the permanent organization as set up. On this point there is no indication that the Soviet Union is embarked on a "soft" policy in Latin America as against the hard line commonly attributed to Peking.

It may be equally true that the Chinese profited from this first worldwide conference to open a front in an area that they had not exploited. The failure of Chinese activity in several parts of Africa, notably in Burundi and Guinea, plus the collapse of the Algerian conference with the fall of Ben Bella, may have contributed to the intransigence demonstrated at Havana.[17]

The wide gap in interpretation is further illustrated by the conclusion of *U. S. News & World Report* that "for the first time in years communist trouble-making has been organized on a coordinated basis. It was Russia's idea. On this one the Russians and Chinese communists are working together against a common foe: the United States. This is the real meaning of the Tri-Continental Conference of the Solidarity of the Peoples of Asia, Africa and Latin America."[18] The *Washington Post* opined, editorially, that "The Russians jumped aboard the liberation committee to keep up with the militants in world communism. The committee is bound to play a minor role in their policy toward Latin America."[19]

It remains to be seen whether the role of the permanent committee formed to carry out the resolutions of the Conference is to be "minor." This latest example of the Communist united front against the established order is not in the least inconsistent with past Soviet performance. It has become increasingly popular to conceive of the Soviet Union as committed to a uniformly peaceful evolution and a sort of

[16]Dan Kurzman, "Cuba Seen as Gainer in Red Camp Row," January 21, 1966.

[17]*Problèmes africains. Revue de presse hebdomadaire* (Brussels), January 27, 1966, p. 5.

[18]January 31, 1966.

[19]January 24, 1966.

gradual transition from capitalism (or even feudalism in the underdeveloped world) to socialism—whereas China, less experienced in the ways of international Marxism, represents the impatient desire to use violence for the quick achievement of its ends. It should be no surprise that at Havana the Soviet Union certainly did not rule out violence. On the contrary, every line of the declaration confirms the support for movements which seek to attain their objective by violent means. Furthermore, no Latin American Communist party has rejected violence as a technique. Nikita Khrushchev made this abundantly clear when he wrote:

> Revolution by peaceful means is in keeping with the interests of the working class and the masses. But if the ruling class counter revolution with force and are unwilling to bow to the will of the people, the proletariat must break their resistance and start a resolute civil war.[20]

The stridency of the Havana conference and its unrestrained demagoguery may very well reflect the increasing concern of the Soviet Union in the face of American policy. The concrete achievements of numerous aspects of the Alliance for Progress and the stepping up of American social and economic commitments in agriculture, education, and social change cannot fail to provoke a reaction on the part of the Soviets. Cuba is the one solid beachhead of the Soviet Union in Latin America. It is a costly one. Cuban leadership has made it very clear that its own survival depends realistically on the extension of revolutionary action elsewhere in the continent.

Latin American Reaction to the Conference

The reaction of the rest of Latin America to the Conference has been vocal and violent. President Raúl Leoni of Venezuela summed it up by saying:

> Venezuela considers that the Tri-Continental Conference presages new aggression against the internal peace of the democratic countries of Latin America. Aggression is in fact the precise objective of the conference.[21]

---

[20]N. S. Khrushchev, "For New Victories for the World Communist Movement," *Kommunist,* p. 73. Quoted in Richard V. Allen, *Peaceful Coexistence: A Communist Blueprint for Victory* (Chicago, 1964), p. 65.

[21]*Washington Daily News,* January 10, 1966.

The Organization of American States took cognizance of the meeting when Peru presented a denunciation of the Soviet Union for encouraging hemisphere guerrilla warfare. This proposal was supported by seventeen other American states. One of the salient items in the resolution was that for the first time the Soviet Union has gone on record, at a public conference, as favorable to armed revolutionary struggle in specifically named Latin American countries.[22]

A few days later the OAS adopted a resolution condemning foreign support of subversive movements as a violation of nonintervention and a threat to the peace and security of the Western Hemisphere. Mexico and Chile abstained in voting on this text, not because of opposition to the intention but on the legal ground of an alleged lack of authority to so act.[23] It is symptomatic of the deep concern of the Latin American governments that the matter was also taken to the United Nations—an unusual step that reflects the gravity with which the new promise of aggression is viewed. The charges were made in a letter to the Security Council. The reaction of Cuba was instantaneous. The Prime Minister wrote that the governments in whose name the letter was signed were "servile instruments of Yankee imperialism in Latin America." He asserted, moreover, that "the people have the right to sweep away, and sooner or later will sweep away, these governments which are treacherous and serve foreign interests in their own countries and they will sweep them away by means of the most violent revolutionary action."[24]

The Conference has given birth apparently to an extraordinary innovation in international law and practice. Intervention is not intervention if it is to assist those who wish to "sweep away" governments deemed reactionary and oppressive. This is clearly a declaration of intention to pursue the process of violent revolution without regard to the rules of international conduct.

Castro and China

Fidel Castro's address on the eve of the Tri-Continental Conference had indicated that all was not harmonious in the relations of his regime and Peking. He complained publicly that China's reduction

---

[22]*The Washington Post,* January 25, 1966.
[23]*The New York Times,* February 3, 1966.
[24]*The New York Times,* February 12, 1966.

of rice exports to Cuba was indicative, in his eyes, of bad faith. This was mild compared with Castro's tirade against the Chinese in a speech published February 7, 1966. The anti-Peking invective would indicate that Castro could no longer be a silent spectator in the Sino-Soviet dispute—especially in light of the frequent speculation that Castro was the coming pro-Peking leader of hemispheric communism and was perhaps impatient with his subservience to the Soviet Union.

From the point of view of economic assistance and material aid there is no doubt that China can provide extremely little to keep the Cuban economy afloat. The rejection of the Soviet Union and its massive support for dubious dependence on far-off China would obviously be suicidal. The language of Castro's denunciation was singularly unbridled. After insisting on the need for absolute solidarity to combat imperialism and the grave danger of a split in the ranks of the revolution, Castro charged the Chinese with "mass distribution of propaganda in our country" particularly among army officers and civil servants. The Chinese were also charged with seeking to establish direct contact with numerous members of the armed forces.[25] The Cuban leader called attention to a previous protest of September 14, 1965, against the propaganda coercion for which he claims the Chinese were responsible. "We very clearly told the representative of the Chinese government that these methods and procedures were exactly the same as the ones used by the United States embassy." China is then charged with "slander," "insolence," and "complete scorn for our country." Peking is further denounced as employing extortionist methods in its trade relations. Although the curtailment of rice exports and tendentious propaganda were to be condemned, the fundamental issue, according to Castro, was whether in the world of tomorrow the powerful nations could presume to blackmail, extort, pressure, attack, and strangle the small countries. China was arraigned as guilty on these counts on the basis of "piracy," "oppression," and "filibusterism."

This remarkable speech, shrill and immoderate in tone, came on the heels of the Tri-Continental Conference. It was difficult at the

[25]*The New York Times,* February 7, 1966, containing numerous excerpts from Castro's speech.

time to judge if this meant a definitive break between Cuba and China, or if it responded to understandings not revealed in the public statements and official documents.

Cuba has certainly become a recognized center for Communist conquest of the Americas and has long been associated with subversive activity everywhere in the hemisphere. With the participation of Communist-controlled governments and the innumerable movements for violence everywhere in the world, Cuba's subversive policy has been elevated to a new level. It was the wedding of the apparatus of communism as a state with the irresponsible terrorist elements which are active on three continents. It is the plainest confirmation of the thesis that the assault on the capitalist stronghold can best be carried out through the "soft underbelly" of Asia, Africa, and Latin America.

PART THREE

IMPLICATIONS FOR U.S. POLICY

Introduction

ALTHOUGH THE SINO-SOVIET CONFLICT HAS RAGED ON VARIOUS CONTINENTS AND IN NUMEROUS COUNTRIES, IT IS NOWHERE CONTESTED MORE FIERCELY THAN ON THE CONTINENT OF ASIA. Indeed, the enormous significance of the split comes most sharply into focus in this vast region, largely because of the war in Vietnam. I say this with deep conviction after five extended Congressional study missions to Asia since 1953, the most recent one completed in late fall of 1965. These tours, four of which have included Vietnam, impress upon me the importance of understanding what it is that continues to divide the Soviets and Chinese in Asia. For here is the crucial battleground not just between ourselves and the Communists but between the Communists themselves.

If there is one driving wedge that separates Russia and China, it is their differing concepts of international change—differences most manifest in Vietnam. The war in that unhappy land, and America's growing military role there, has undoubtedly done more to shatter any hopes of a Sino-Soviet reconciliation than any other recent factor. Secretary of State Dean Rusk told our subcommittee: "North Vietnam may be important in the Communist world at the present time more because of its effect on the struggle between the two leaders than—at this stage, anyhow—because of a problem of relations between the Communist world as a whole and the free world."

Some experts have warned that increased pressure by the United

States in Vietnam might draw Russia and Red China together in common cause, at least until the "imperialists" could be defeated in Vietnam. Thus far, quite the reverse has fortunately occurred. As our engagement in the war has intensified, so has the split. While I was in Asia during November 1965, Peking angrily charged in a party journal that the Russians were helping Washington find a way to end the war through negotiations. After three days of ominous silence while the Kremlin obviously considered what to do, Moscow struck back with the bluntest attack ever aimed at Red China. It bitterly castigated the article as "full of impermissible, utterly groundless, slanderous, provocative fabrications, permeated with a spirit of hostility toward the Soviet people and toward the Communist Party of the Soviet Union."

From my discussions in the Far East with our officials and numerous Asian leaders, one fact continues to emerge. The Chinese and Soviets, each employing his own tactics, are increasingly competing for power and influence in Asia. This helps to explain Sino-Soviet hostility revolving around Vietnam. The Soviets have actually been giving more military assistance to North Vietnam than the Chinese—supplies, arms, anti-aircraft missiles. And I have no doubt that Moscow's emissaries in Hanoi are reminding the North Vietnamese that Soviet support amounts to *more* than words. This infuriates and frustrates the Chinese Communists who are sensitive to the sarcastic criticism that they are backing Vietnam only down to the last North Vietnamese—not down to the last Chinese.

Make no mistake, we are not about to see the end of Sino-Soviet friction and deep conflict in Asia no matter what happens in Vietnam. The Chinese loudly announced, in the now famous 30,000-word statement by Marshal Lin Piao, that their strategy is to encircle the industrial states by first conquering the underdeveloped world. This is in the same pattern as their takeover of China and in stark contrast to the Soviet Union's basic goal of concentrating on the advanced industrial states of the West. Yet we must not conclude that the Soviets are incapable of rural activity or that the Chinese are so rigid that they cannot engage in subversive activities in the urban power centers of Asia.

All this leads to a central question: What can the United States do about the Sino-Soviet dispute? This question cuts to the core of one of the great foreign policy issues of our day, if not the decade. There can be no simple, quick answers, but it is clear that no issue so challenges the wisdom of our leaders. No issue so puts to the test the skill and judgment of our governmental foreign policy machinery and intelligence apparatus. Every citizen should be well aware of this, for the momentous division in the ranks of our Communist adversaries offers both enormous possibilities and pitfalls for ourselves and the free world. And the stakes are far too high for us to make bad decisions. That is precisely why our subcommittee considered it crucial to find broad answers to questions such as these: Should the United States actively attempt to widen the conflict? Or should we maintain a strictly "hands off" position? To what, if any, degree should we attempt to tailor our policies to reap benefits from the Communist policies?

I believe it would be the sheerest folly for us to do literally nothing. As a matter of survival and reality we must gear our policies to the conflict. In every area of the world today we must decide how best to proceed within the framework of Soviet-Chinese maneuvering. Sometimes as a matter of *decision* we should stand away from the infighting. In other instances I believe there may be openings into which we can move swiftly and astutely in order to achieve vital advancements in our own interest.

There is a range of options. For example, as a result of the conflict there is a strong tide in parts of Eastern Europe against Soviet *domination*. We must be extremely careful in our relationships with the Soviet bloc nations not to endanger or discourage this tide. In Latin America where Chinese "militant" factions push for more guerrilla activity, we must not be lulled into believing that the Soviet-directed "nonactivist" parties are necessarily less dangerous.

Johnson Administration officials have warned against taking comfort from the dispute. I strongly agree. Moreover, I am convinced that we must be continually alert for ways to strengthen our own position when weaknesses appear in the Communist camp because of the split. In the Dominican Republic, for example, there has been friction and distrust between the pro-Soviet and the pro-Chinese groups. Although these two factions joined forces during last spring's revolt, they have since gone back to quarreling over what strategy will be best for gaining control of the country. Surely this gives the United States more breathing room in which it can strengthen moderate, anti-Communist elements, especially among the youth whose sympathies the Communists have often captured, not only in the Dominican Republic but throughout Latin America.

Above all, a rigid, all-inclusive policy toward the conflict is needed. What our officials must be able and willing to do is act decisively according to various world regions and various political situations. It could be calamitous if our policies abroad were put into a strait jacket of strict rules. At the same time, nothing could be worse than for our diplomats to be frozen by a "do-nothing" policy—which has been known to happen. For these reasons I wish to emphasize that the Sino-Soviet schism puts our officials and our government agencies to the severest test of their abilities. The challenge of the Sino-Soviet conflict is worthy of the Nation's finest minds. With this thought, let us now consider the views of six eminent authorities on the meaning of the dispute for U.S. foreign policy.

C. J. Z.

1. An American Initiative in East Europe

—*ZBIGNIEW K. BRZEZINSKI*

The Sino-Soviet dispute has fractured irretrievably the unity of the international Communist movement. Throughout the world numerous factions are contesting against one another and at the same time they are asserting their independence either of Moscow's or Peking's control. This has given the East European states increased room for maneuver, while decreasing the vitality and unity of the Communist ideology. Gaining the support of the East European parties against China has become important to the Soviet Union, but it has been purchased at an increasingly higher price. The East European states have been able not only to increase their autonomy in internal affairs but have been able even to defy the Soviet Union.

A New International Context

The Sino-Soviet dispute has also had a very direct impact on the Soviet Union itself. It is contributing to the erosion of Communist ideology; it is pushing the Soviet leaders into a more moderate, although still hostile, attitude toward the West; and it is prompting a gradual process of "Europeanization" of Russia. Russia is increasingly identifying itself with Europe and is beginning to view China as a major national threat.

While the Soviet and East European Communists still view the West as an adversary, they are increasingly interested in some limited accommodation and are more inclined—especially after the Cuban confrontation—to seek international stability, particularly in Europe. This is dictated in part by their own internal economic difficulties and by their need for trade with the West.

All of this, cumulatively, creates an altogether new international context. In East Europe, too, domestic pressures are being more strongly felt, and these pressures generally are in favor of greater stability. At the same time, nationalism is beginning to make its appearance felt and is gradually transforming the present Communist dictatorships into a mixture of nationalist-Communist-technocratic authoritarianisms. The regimes governing the East European states have inescapably become preoccupied with their own national interests —creating in turn a more favorable setting for Western policy and initiatives.

Proposal for an American Initiative: A "Johnson Plan"

These trends have special implications for American policy. In Asia, the United States should continue to resist vigorously any further Communist aggression: failure to do so would even invigorate the waning revolutionary aspirations among the East European and Soviet Communists. In Europe, the preconditions for an eventual reconciliation are increasing because of trends in nationalism, internal economic difficulties, and other effects of the Sino-Soviet split.

De Gaulle has taken advantage of these trends to proclaim a policy of a "European Europe." The United States should preempt de Gaulle's policy by seizing the initiative in attempting to reunite Europe. Otherwise there is a great danger that America may cease to be relevant to a Europe increasingly dominated by narrow nationalisms, including that of the frustrated, divided Germany, increasingly dissatisfied with the declaratory American policy on the subject of reunification.

By taking the initiative in developing policies designed to bring both Russia and East Europe into closer relationships with the West, thereby to end the European partition, America would be furthering its own basic interests. First of all, the very fact of such a commitment would do much to revive America's waning importance to Europe. Secondly, it would provide a framework for restoring the East European nations to independence without simultaneously creating new instabilities or stimulating narrow nationalisms. Finally, by laying the foundations for a broader East-West settlement, it would eliminate the persisting European fears of an American-Soviet power duopoly. All that would be consistent with domestic American values and the American quest for world order.

The American initiative should be designed:

1. To convince the East Europeans, particularly the Czechs and the Poles, that East Germany limits their freedom without enhancing their security. This will involve greater contacts with the East Europeans while isolating further the East Germans.
2. To promote German-Polish reconciliation, somewhat on the model of Franco-German reconciliation in the fifties. This will require an American declaration that the present Oder-Neisse frontier will be recognized formally and finally at the very moment that Germany is reunified. This should be promised in advance.
3. To minimize the Russian fear of Germany. This does not mean military disengagement, which in any case is no longer feasible, but the willingness of West Germany to assure the Russians that under no circumstances will it ever seek a national nuclear deterrent.
4. To relate the expansion of economic ties to more extensive cultural and social contacts in order to undermine the narrow ideological perspectives of the ruling Communist elites and to avoid a situation whereby close economic relations are merely used by these elites to resolve their economic difficulties.

5. To promote multilateral ties with West Europe and in East Europe. As direct Soviet control wanes and as East European nationalism, even under Communist leadership, reasserts itself, it should be an explicit goal of American policy to promote multilateral political and economic reasons, lest East Europe—and even all of Europe—become Balkanized.

The pursuit of these goals would be facilitated and accelerated by a dramatic proposal for a general all-European economic development designed to cut across the present partition, to narrow the existing disparities in European standards of living, to reduce economic and political significance of the existing frontiers, and to promote greater intercourse in both trade and human contacts through the development of an all-European system of communications. An American initiative to that end and American participation in such a venture are particularly desirable for the sake of America's continued relevance to Europe. Such a proposal could create the preconditions for a reconciliation of East and West in Europe or, at the very least, it would create a magnetic attraction for a great many East European nations and eventually perhaps for Russia as well.

This initiative will require a fundamental reassessment of the American position in Europe and of the American relationship to Europe. The central point is that America is becoming less vital to a divided but secure West Europe faced by an increasingly independent East Europe; it was essential to a divided and insecure West Europe faced by a united Soviet bloc. Accordingly, America must address itself to the key European problem—the partition of Europe. Even if the United States fails to resolve that partition, the very fact of taking a peaceful initiative with respect to it will help to reestablish America's pertinence to Europe.

2. The "Third World"

—BERNARD B. FALL

As of 1966 the Sino-Soviet split was a fact which no country in the world could simply ignore. But so was, on the other hand, the cooperation—albeit reluctant and in the face of constant mutual recrimination—between the Soviet Union and the Chinese People's Republic in providing a minimum of military assistance to North Vietnam. The Vietnam war has condemned the two major Communist powers to work together, in at least this instance, like unwilling partners in a "three-legged race." For they both have much to lose in Vietnam: in the case of Russia, her credibility as the guarantor of the military integrity of the whole Communist power system; and in the case of Communist China, her credibility as a discoverer of a politico-military strategy capable of leapfrogging the nuclear status quo.

There is nothing new in the cooperation between reluctant partners in a situation which affects their overall position. Some striking examples are the cooperation between Britain, France, and Israel in the Suez Canal campaign of November 1956; or French President de Gaulle's support of the United States in the 1962 Cuban crisis. This cautionary note should be kept in mind, for the following pages must be understood in the context of a *continuing* Sino-Soviet split and, hopefully, not in the context of a situation in which American pressures in the

Far East will have provided the shotgun to a renewed Sino-Soviet wedding. An amicable resolution of the Sino-Soviet split—regardless of whether it is due to a change of leaders in either or both countries or to an external situation—would completely change relations between the free world and the Communist orbit. It would force an immediate reevaluation of United States relations with the vast areas of the "Third World"—the uncommitted nations of Latin America, Africa, and Asia.

The present effects of the split have been amply discussed by other contributors: Soviet emphasis on coexistence in Europe and in Cuba; Sino-Soviet competition in the nonaligned countries; struggle for influence in southeast Asian countries such as Indonesia, Cambodia, and North Vietnam. The assets that both antagonists can commit to that struggle for influence in the "Third World" are far from negligible: on the one hand, Soviet military and economic technology; and, on the other, China's incredible ability at low-level organization for revolutionary warfare and manpower-based development. In addition, the Chinese can argue that their path leads to liberation from the White Man's tutelage, regardless of whether the White Man in question represents the British Raj, the United States, or Moscow.

As Ambassador George F. Kennan judiciously points out, this internecine struggle is not necessarily a unilateral benefit to the West; and neither would be an aggravation of East-West tensions over the basically peripheral Vietnam issue to the point where, in his words, "we force the Russians back into a closer relation with the Chinese, or even into an intense and exclusive competition with the Chinese for leadership in the destruction of our world position." In this fairly narrow area between the worldwide aggravations of an ever widening Sino-Soviet split and of a sudden re-coalescence of the two major Communist powers into a single (even if temporary) bloc, American policy planners will have to steer a deliberate course over largely uncharted seas.

This is nowhere more evident than in the Asian rim areas bordering on Communist China.

The Asian Rim Area

At present the countries of the Asian rim area are most likely to both benefit and suffer from the Sino-Soviet split. Most of them—

Pakistan, India, Nepal, Ceylon, Burma, Indonesia, Laos, and Cambodia —are directly represented in Peking and Moscow, and many of them have in some form accepted North Vietnamese representatives. Even anti-Communist Thailand is host to a large Soviet embassy. In fact, only Malaya and the Philippines have no official relations with Communist states.

Aggravation of the split puts a serious strain on all the Asian rim countries—except Thailand and Malaya which rely entirely on Western aid and protection (American in the case of Thailand, British in the case of Malaya and the city-state of Singapore). The agonizing choice between an economically beneficial policy of coexistence and a more or less veiled hostility with nearby Communist China is a decision none of the rim countries feels can be made lightly. Hence the recent pressures by statesmen from such countries, directly or indirectly, in favor of diplomatic solutions to the major overt conflict involving the United States and the key protagonists of the Sino-Soviet split.

Thus far, "aid races" between Russia and China have not taken place to any major extent in the area. "Arms races," on the other hand, have and are in fact continuing in such countries as India, Pakistan, Indonesia, Cambodia, and North Vietnam. They are likely to continue in one form or another throughout the area, although at least in Laos the split between the pro-Communist Pathet-Lao forces and the neutralist forces of General Kong-Lê (with the latter now backing the coalition government of Prince Souvanna Phouma) has resulted in the only total elimination of a Soviet military aid program (to Kong-Lê) in favor of a Sino–North Vietnamese program entirely reserved for the Pathet-Lao forces. In some cases—notably Indonesia, Cambodia, and Pakistan—Western and Chinese military aid programs coexist: in Indonesia, U.S. C-130 transport aircraft are used by troops with Chinese small arms; in Pakistan, Chinese-built tanks and fighters mingle with similar U.S. Military Assistance Program (MAP) equipment; and in Cambodia, Chinese light weapons, Soviet MIGs, and French armor and French-donated U.S.-built aircraft operate side by side.

What all this means in terms of future American policy for southeast Asia is still hard to fathom, although in some areas (Pakistan and Indonesia notably) the outlines of a new policy approach are becoming evident. A brief area-by-area survey may provide some indications:

1. The Indian Subcontinent. There are legitimate border conflicts in the whole area. *Both* Peking and Taiwan argue (and this is probably the only point on which they wholly agree) that the so-called "McMahon Line" demarcating the Sino-Indian boundary is a colonial border imposed by Britain upon a prostrate China. And the record will show that India has over the past two decades been reluctant to discuss the boundary with her neighbor.

The same legitimacy is true for the Kashmir border question, which has been left in abeyance since 1948 and has been the object of sporadic fighting and dispute ever since. That the case is far from being wholly one-sided is evident from the single UN vote on the subject: in 1957 when India decided to integrate Kashmir into her territory, the Security Council voted 10-0 asking India to desist from the measure (which she refused to do). Russia abstained from voting.

While the Sino-Indian border issue affects American policy only inasmuch as it inclines India to be more acutely aware of Communist Chinese aggressiveness, it affects the Sino-Soviet split quite seriously. The USSR has apparently made up her mind to continue supporting India—not only for the pragmatic reason that between Pakistan and India the latter is the more important friend to have, but also for the ideological reason that its help to India keeps Red China in check in an important area of the world.

The situation in Pakistan is the one most likely to give the United States trouble in the not-too-distant future. On paper, Pakistan is still an American ally in both the Southeast Asia Treaty Organization (SEATO) and the Central Treaty Organization (CENTO). In fact, it constitutes the linking member between the two treaty groups. Pakistan also controls strategic ground in the Himalayas and the best access routes to landlocked neutral Afghanistan. What Pakistan considers to have been the United States' failure to take Pakistan's side in the Pakistan-Indian armed conflict of September-October 1965 has been instrumental in orienting Pakistan's course in favor of Peking. To a certain extent, however, that course had already been adopted somewhat earlier and the absence of a Russian "option" has quasi-automatically thrown the game to Communist China at this particular juncture. Chinese military equipment delivered to Pakistan was shown in military parades there in the spring of 1966, and a Pakistan Air Lines flight (operating U.S.-made Boeing 707s) connects Karachi with Shanghai.

However, Pakistan has not yet allowed existing treaty relations with the United States to lapse altogether; in fact, a warming trend has become evident. Within the Sino-Soviet split, nevertheless, the situation represents a net victory for the Chinese People's Republic: it opens a "crack" in the American treaty system in the so-called "Northern Tier," introduces Chinese personnel into an area where China is notably lacking in legal footholds, and embarrasses the USSR in her own relations with the Moslem world.

It is doubtful, however, that the near future will offer the United States much opportunity for maneuver. American popularity in India is always a volatile affair and subject to rapid and unforeseen changes. And so, for that matter, is Red Chinese popularity in Pakistan. An equitable settlement of the Indo-Pakistan dispute is likely to be of more durable profit to the United States than the present highly unstable equilibrium.

Mention should be made of the potentially troublesome situation in the Himalayan region, where the small states of Nepal and Bhutan maintain a precarious existence. Chinese aid projects, notably in building road connections between China and the border states, add to the vulnerability of India. A greater measure of clearly disinterested aid on the part of the U.S. may be helpful in reestablishing a proper balance. The Nagaland guerrilla war, which has plagued India's northeastern frontier for more than a decade, is still a limited war and thus far devoid of Chinese influence. If this were to change, India's position in the northeastern corner of the subcontinent might well become highly unstable and might affect Burma as well.

In sum, the whole subcontinent subsists at present on an unstable plateau of countervailing forces. But more than almost anywhere else, chances are slim for a reconciliation of China with her main antagonist there, India; and chances of continued Russian support of India are excellent. This may assure the United States of a certain amount of leeway and provide her with the possibility of engaging in creative policies of her own.

2. *Southeast Asia.* In southeast Asia, with its 250 million people and vast resources, the Vietnam war overshadows all other develop-

ments and distorts all perspectives. As of mid-1966, it is impossible to project the implications of *anything* the USSR or China might do in the way of supporting North Vietnam in her own struggle against American airpower, or in her own operation in support of the South Vietnamese insurgency.

It is painfully obvious that the extremes—a flat American withdrawal or a "twenty-divisions-for-twenty-years" commitment—could yield just about equally painful results in terms of future implications. And it is obvious that any intermediate solution involving negotiation with the adversary will in turn reflect more or less adversely on the United States.

Yet it is also in southeast Asia that a sudden change in the Sino-Soviet dispute (for the worse or the better) could have equally dangerous results. A total split would compel the USSR to choose between alternatives: (1) stopping all aid to North Vietnam that transits via China—relying entirely on American-controlled sealanes and subject to risks like those of the Cuban blockade; or (2) simply and purely abandoning North Vietnam to its fate—just as the Greek or Malay guerrillas were abandoned, but as no full-fledged Communist state ever was. Conversely, a sudden rapprochement between the bloc powers would leave the United States and associated forces in Vietnam completely exposed to overwhelming enemy ground forces—all of a sudden enjoying almost complete technological parity with the United States. Or, more subtly and therefore more devastatingly perhaps (and this was suggested by the Chinese, for example, in *Jen-min Jih-pao* of January 5, 1966), the USSR could increase pressures on the United States in such remote places as Berlin and Turkey, thereby adding not only to the military burden of the United States but also to the already existing strains in the NATO alliance.

That this possibility is by no means far-fetched is best illustrated by the fact that in late 1965 Red China openly admitted that she had refused the Soviet Union base rights in South China, near the North Vietnamese border, where the USSR apparently had wanted to station several squadrons of her first-line MIG-23 jet fighters as early as a few weeks after the onset of U.S. bombing operations against North Vietnam. Such a situation, had it materialized, would have put to American policymakers the agonizing decision of risking direct clashes with the Soviets. If such a situation has thus far been avoided, it is in large measure due to the total intransigence of the Chinese and *not*—contrary to what often seems to be believed—to the Soviet intention to refrain from coming to the succor of North Vietnam and to avoid any kind of clash with the United States at all costs. After all, the surface-to-air (SAM) missile bases in North Vietnam directly involve the USSR, and Soviet technicians must be among the casualties of the destroyed SAM sites, just as there are American pilots among those shot down by SAMs over North Vietnam.

It is clear that the conclusion from any such overview of the present Vietnamese situation (regardless of the *internal* South Vietnamese situation, which only in small part is influenced by the Sino-Soviet dispute) can only be that a further escalation of the Vietnam conflict can hardly be construed as likely to have a mollifying influence on the Sino-Soviet dispute. But in my view there are still very good chances for a (even if temporary) Soviet "hard" position with regard to Vietnam rather than a conversion of Hanoi or Peking to a more conciliatory stand.

In the meantime, however, the Sino-Soviet dispute has put an almost total "freeze" on Communist reactions to such problems as Indonesia's virtual destruction of the PKI, the largest Communist Party outside the Communist orbit. This event has already diminished pressures upon neighboring Malaysia of Indonesia's "crush-Malaysia" campaign, thus lightening Britain's defense burden there. It will in all likelihood permit a careful and low-keyed rapprochement between the United States and the new leadership in Indonesia—although it must be clearly understood that any overplaying of that approach may have the entirely opposite effect on the extremely sensitive Indonesian public opinion. At present, its mood is as much generally xenophobic as it is anti-PKI.

In the western segment of southeast Asia (Malaya, Thailand, and Burma) the present setbacks suffered by Red China may lead to a more aggressive rather than a more conservative Chinese policy, since the Peking leaders might seek to recoup their losses in other vulnerable areas. All pretenses to the contrary notwithstanding, Thailand *is* vulnerable to subversion—not only because of infiltrations from Laos, but simply because of twenty years of dormancy in such key fields as social and political reforms in an otherwise rapidly changing geographic area. To the south, the fate of the Chinese-populated state of Singapore, which stands vulnerably alone after its break with Malaya at the latter's initiative, cannot be fathomed. Even slight changes in the economic balance may tilt volatile Singaporean politics into unforeseeable directions. Burma, under the leadership of General Ne Win, seems to attempt disengagement from the present political problems in the area through a policy amounting to an isolationism almost matching that of Japan in the early nineteenth century. This has permitted her to avoid entanglement in the Sino-Soviet dispute. As long as Burma stays on her present course, an American policy of wisdom will be leaving Burma alone, particularly after the still burning issue of the American-supplied Chinese Nationalist guerrillas of General Li-Mi who haunted the Sino-Burmese border areas.

Some observers have tended to attribute the present disarray of the Communist forces in southeast Asia to the presence of a large number of American troops in South Vietnam. In my view, this is making short shrift of the always present aero-naval strength of the U.S. Seventh Fleet and the American bases in the Philippines, Taiwan, and Okinawa. These forces, for example, could in any case block Chinese help to, say, PKI guerrillas in Indonesia. In fact, it could well be argued that the continued bogging down of a quarter-million American troops in Vietnam, in the face of a lightly armed enemy, can hardly be considered encouraging when it is remembered, for example, how much ground was covered by American troops under similar terrain (but not political) conditions during the Pacific campaigns of World War II.[1]

In projecting the implications of present events in southeast Asia, it will be important not to confuse cause and effect of the Western position in relation to the Sino-Soviet split. Little can be gained by attributing to Western acumen or fortitude what in effect was little else than a Communist mistake of monumental proportions—although

---

[1]To give one numerical example, during *all* of World War II, the United States expended a total of 680,000 tons of bombs throughout the Pacific Theater. In 1965, the U.S. expended 255,000 tons of bombs over the 127,000 square miles of North and South Vietnam and plans (according to Secretary of Defense Robert S. McNamara) to expend 638,000 tons of bombs in 1966. If that schedule is adhered to, Vietnam will have been hit with more bombs (by 35 per cent) in two years than the whole Pacific Theater—including highly industrialized Manchuria and Japan—in four years.

there is comfort in the sheer fact that Communists *do* make mistakes, just like everybody else.

3. *The Far East.* At the northern rim of non-Communist Asia, Japan looms as a future problem area; but on the surface its problems have little to do with the Sino-Soviet split.

It is nevertheless a fact that the economic quasi-blockade which the USSR has clamped on China as a result of the split has resulted in Japan's vastly increased interest in the Chinese market and China's strong interest in improved relations with Japan. Economic missions of both countries have exchanged visits, and some commercial agreements were made, though not yet of a volume sufficient to modify Japanese trade patterns established over the past two decades.

However, increased marketing problems for Japanese products in the West (notably in the United States) might in the long run make the Chinese market more attractive to Japan. This may give the Chinese a certain amount of political leverage as well. It must be realized, however, that for a long time to come China will find it difficult to come up with the extensive amounts of hard currency necessary to make the market attractive to Japanese business interests—particularly if China must also find the hard currency necessary to buy several million tons of foodstuffs in the West every year to make up for its own huge deficits in food production.

Inasmuch as the Sino-Soviet split has provided the Chinese with an incentive to build their own nuclear arsenal (one which is not under Soviet control), Japan is the country most likely to have to fear China's development of even a modest delivery capability. That fact of itself should douse many of the hopes expressed in some Japanese circles that a slow "divorce" from a too-tight relation with the United States might contribute to a rapid normalization of relations with Peking.

Barring any unforeseen deterioration of Japan's internal economics, the Sino-Soviet split is not likely to affect Japan too deeply one way or the other. Thus the split is not likely to exert an adverse pressure on American relations with Japan. There are many specifically Nippo-American issues (Okinawa, trade, etc.) which are of far greater importance to both countries and which are likely to be exploited by communism regardless of the split.

The Split in Africa

The half-decade between 1960 and 1966 does not seem to have been propitious to communism in Africa, and the Sino-Soviet split does not seem to have had much influence there, inasmuch as neither the USSR nor the CPR can claim to have made notable gains at the expense of each other. Nor have they, for that matter, been noticeably better treated when local African regimes decided to dispense with the bulk of the Sino-Soviet presence in their respective countries. In those countries where the expulsion of Chinese experts seemed more conspicuous, apparently it was mainly a case (as in Ghana) of there being more Chinese to expel. In almost no area did the Russians inherit positions lost or vacated by the Chinese, except perhaps in a few isolated cases in East Africa.

Perhaps it is still too early to tell what caused the wave of anti-Communist and, in many instances, specifically anti-Chinese reactions in Black Africa. Plain racism cannot be excluded altogether in some places. In some other places (like Burundi) the Chinese were extremely clumsy in intervening in internal affairs because they were unfamiliar with African ways and people and, in many cases, they were unable to deliver the goods promised in their aid programs or to deliver them in promised quantity or quality.

But the key reason for the Sino-Soviet setbacks in Africa, both south of the Sahara and in the "Maghreb" (Arabic North Africa) was the unwillingness of the Africans to become active partners in the Sino-Soviet quarrel. The wrecking of the "Bandung II" conference (which was to have been held in 1965 in Algeria) was due in large measure to the Chinese decision to make the seating of the Soviet Union a test case of the loyalties of the whole Third World. But the representatives of the nonaligned states refused to draw their feelings that clearly, particularly over an issue in which they had no particular stake and which to many of them was little more than a "ferocious theological brawl—unlike anything that has been seen since the Reformation."[2]

This has not been a unilateral blessing for the United States, however, since some of the Afro-Arabic nations seem in fact to resent the

---

[2]John P. Roche, "Containing China," *Commentary* (May 1966).

lack of counterpoise to the United States which the split in the Sino-Soviet bloc represents to them. That is exactly what President Nasser expressed on May 9, 1966 (on the eve of the arrival of Soviet Premier Kosygin in Egypt) when he blamed the split on the "imperialist pressures [exerted] everywhere on the world's liberation movements."[3]

It is clear, however, that the Sino-Soviet split has perhaps had its most emphatic effect in Africa precisely because the local Communist movements were so weak and thus relied more heavily on the presence of the foreign Communist missions in order to create at least a friendly atmosphere for themselves. The departure of those missions has in most places created a small void which in most cases has been replaced by expanded Western assistance programs. The trend seems to be a favorable upswing for the United States and the ex-colonial powers of the area.

But it must be realized that even a slight mishandling of the Rhodesian crisis or of the other smoldering problems of undivided White Man's rule in the south of Africa can reverse such trends fairly quickly.

Latin America

Time is running out for the United States all over Latin America. Thanks to internal problems in the area, the Sino-Soviet split appears to work in favor of further revolutionary activism there, despite the obvious setback suffered by China during the Anti-Imperialist Conference of Havana in the spring of 1966.

This is easily explainable. Although for reasons of geography and obvious economic and military weakness over the distances involved China—standing isolated through the split—can hardly provide a *physical* alternative to Soviet support, Chinese politico-military views are obviously nearer to what Latin American revolutionaries like to consider the "concrete requirements of the situation." As the guerrilla movements in Venezuela, Colombia, Peru, and Bolivia clearly show, Latin American revolutionary movements for the most part accept the basically Chinese theory that, regardless of immediate or even proximate success, every movement requires what is called a *foco*. This is an overt center of insurrection in which a small group of militants will learn the basics of guerrilla action and will in turn be

---

[3]*New York Times,* May 10, 1966.

trained to become the cadres of a possible wider insurrection.

That view, in light of the obvious past failures of most "reformist" movements in Latin America—Mexico being the exception, and the Chilean Christian Democrats perhaps the last chance of that trend—holds that the Soviet Union can no longer be counted upon to support a "liberation movement" if that support entails the risk of a confrontation with the United States. The Cuban confrontation of 1962 confirmed the view of that school of thought. Nor do revolutionary moderates, such as Dr. Juan Bosch in the Dominican Republic, seem to have much chance of prevailing: the landing of American troops in the Dominican Republic in the spring of 1965 vitiates that aspect.

That leaves little else but a long-range preparation for an eventual revolution based on a combination of guerrilla movements and urban agitation, over an area wide enough to make concentrated military action of the Vietnam type almost impossible. Vietnam, with its 127,000 square miles and 33 million people (both figures include North and South) is a distressing forecast for a similar war fought over the 6 million square miles and 150 million people of South America. Any revolutionary blueprint for this area must be nearer to the three-decade Chinese Communist struggle for power than to the fairly rapid Soviet revolution.

It is not at all surprising that the most perceptive study on the subject, written by an author in full sympathy with its objectives, defines the phenomenon as "Castroism: The Long March of Latin America."[4] Ironically, then, Castroism, whether consciously or not, is far more a child of the Chinese than of the Russian revolution—regardless of whether it currently depends upon Russia for its material support. Hence, a unified Sino-Soviet policy for Latin America would certainly show the effects of Russia's moderating influence, whereas the existence of the open split allows the revolutionary movements in each country a clear choice of what revolutionary "model" to follow. There can be little doubt that the Chinese "Long March" model will prevail, either in its consciously pro-Chinese form or in the modified form of Castroism.

It is in Latin America, precisely because the relatively simple solutions of military force will be largely unapplicable (or politically

[4]Régis Debray, "Le Castrisme: La longue marche de l'Amérique Latine," *Les Temps Modernes,* XX, No. 224 (January 1965).

unacceptable) there, that the most serious tests of American political acumen and flexibility—as advocated by Ambassador Kennan—are likely to come. For I cannot conceive of a Latin American country that will accept B-52 raids on its territory or the long-term commitment of a North American force on its shores, even in the form of an inter-American peace force.

Contrary to the other underdeveloped areas which have been discussed here, the Sino-Soviet split offers little room for comfort in Latin America. If anything, it accelerates the revolutionary polarization process—and, in all likelihood, in favor of the Chinese view of history and of the future. The implications for the United States are obvious: Alliance for Progress and all, American policies in Latin America have become frozen into a set attitude which seems to leave little room for discrimination between one revolutionary movement and another, and even less for recognition of the fact that, regardless of what happens to Castro as a person and Cuba as a country, "Castroism" as a *revolutionary idea* has become a permanent fixture of Latin American political life. As the noted author Hannah Arendt remarked in her excellent book *On Revolution,* the French revolution was a total failure and the American revolution a magnificent success—yet every revolution since the 1790s has imitated the French failure rather than the American success. The same may be true with Castroism. Chinese preoccupation with Vietnam and the Soviet Union has perhaps not yet permitted her to cultivate the fertile bed which awaits her particular ideology in Latin America.

But that Chinese omission offers little room for comfort to future American relations with the sister continent.

In sum, the Sino-Soviet split has tended to favor new openings for a forward-looking American foreign policy in the Indian subcontinent; has created the dangers of further escalation in Vietnam while lessening tensions in Malaya and Indonesia; and has almost created a total void of effective Communist action in much of Africa. In Latin America it has, if anything, made the need for change even more imperative. As in other areas of the world, a quarrel between two allies is not necessarily an unalloyed benefit to the opponent. This is a lesson that both the United States and the Third World must learn from the present aspects of the Sino-Soviet rift.

3. Guidelines for U.S. Policy in East Asia

—*GEORGE E. TAYLOR*

The main lines of present U.S. policy toward Asia and the western Pacific were laid down by President Truman. They are to maintain sufficient military force in the western Pacific to discourage open aggression by the Communist powers and to assist those states that wish to preserve their independence. To further these policies we have concluded bilateral mutual security pacts, as with Japan, Korea, Taiwan, and the Philippines, and multilateral arrangements such as SEATO and ANZUS. Our military power in the western Pacific depends at least to some extent on the viability of these political arrangements—in other words, on the morale, the attitudes, and the endurance of our allies. Where appropriate this calls for U.S. assistance in the construction of the institutions and the spirit of the modern state and nation. More than ever before, the various ways in which our policy is expressed—military, political, economic, psychological—are interdependent.

Nation Building

The weakest links in the chain are the new underdeveloped states (one can hardly call them nations) of southeast Asia. Where we deal with strong nation-states, such as Japan, the lack of integration in policy implementation is often concealed, but not in our dealings with emerging nations, such as Vietnam, which have to collect the materials, choose the design, construct the house, live in it, and defend it all at the same time. To some extent in the Philippines and to a larger degree in southeast Asia, we are inevitably involved in the intimate task of nation building; as the problems of the new nations are all so interrelated, participation in their solution is no simple matter.

Let us remember that the United States brings a considerable amount of experience to the task. Under different conditions, but not so different as to be irrelevant, the United States has been engaged in the business of nation building in the Philippines since 1900 and in Japan since 1945. In the case of the Philippines we contributed the politically decisive concept of a self-liquidating colony; in the case of Japan, the vital assistance in releasing revolutionary forces which were already in being in such a way as to change the internal balance of power in favor of representative government and a free economy. In the Philippines we helped to defeat the Communist-led attempt to seize power not with large military forces but with political ideas and strategies. We have more recently been attempting to devise a body of theory to guide us in our efforts to encourage economic growth in underdeveloped countries—and ideas in this field are likely to be as important as weapons of war. There is a good deal of solid history behind these new dimensions in the implementation of U.S. policy: in fact, the two most important seedbeds—in the Philippines and Japan—were cultivated before the direct impact of Communist power in eastern Asia.

The effect of the Sino-Soviet bloc, divided or not, upon the U.S. position is felt most keenly in those areas where the state structure and national sentiment are the weakest. The invasion of South Korea, for example, led to a continuing effort to fabricate a nation out of South Korea. It also led to the addition of a new psychological warfare device of nonforcible repatriation of prisoners of war—a valuable tool in combating Communist powers. To the Communists we also owe the clause in SEATO which authorizes a member state to call for help not only against direct aggression but also against internal subversion—a very important addition to the legal armory and a timely recognition of the political facts of life.

Most significant of all, perhaps, the Communists have forced us to pay attention to what is now called counterinsurrection, a type of civil war which Mao Tse-tung has made famous and in which he has had some successes. The Communists have forced on us the most painful of all tasks—the task of creative thinking. The struggles against Communist terrorists in Malaya and the Philippines succeeded because the governments saw the problem as a whole, as a sort of social, political, and military continuum. They formulated doctrines for countering civil war; they made military action an integral part of political and social action. They won because of the superiority of their ideas, institutions, and organizations. From these experiences, as from experience in Vietnam, we have learned that we have to clarify our objectives in order to coordinate the means by which they are to be achieved.

Chinese Objectives

Does the conflict between Moscow and Peking change the situation described above? Basically, in my opinion, it does not, but it leads to several modifications which are important. First of all let us say something about Chinese Communist policy. Communist China has three main objectives: The first is to finish the civil war. It is essential for Peking to eliminate the political influence of the National Government of China if control of the mainland is to be secure. She has tried to do this by force, by subversion, and by getting the U.N. General Assembly to do it for her. She has tried to get Moscow's assistance not only in the United Nations but also in the Taiwan Straits. It is possible that the conflict has reduced the chances of war in this area. Second, Peking seeks to establish China as a great power—certainly on a regional basis by industrialization, by development of nuclear capacity, and by expansion of her influence beyond Chinese borders. Third, Peking seeks to increase its own influence in the bloc—which, in turn, would decrease that of the Soviet Union. Her method is to undermine the ideological prestige of the Soviet leaders; to capture—by means of an organizational drive—as many of the worldwide Communist parties as possible; and to oppose every sign of agreement between Moscow and the United States, however flimsy. As the facts of nuclear power force the Soviet Union, for its own safety, into some measures of arms control, Peking has the propaganda advantage. Pursuit of the third objective (increasing Chinese influence within the bloc) has led to a vigorous expansion of Chinese activities in Asia, Africa, and Latin America.

Consequences for U.S. Policy

The first consequence for the U.S. position is that the Soviet Union does not loom as large in eastern Asia and the western Pacific as it used to. We can expect to deal more and more exclusively with the Chinese. Second, the difficulties of anticipating Chinese and Soviet reactions have been increased because both Moscow and Peking use the flow of events to pressure each other. We have to guess how far the one is prepared to go in embarrassing the other. In my view it is wiser to assume that if the Communist regime in Peking ever gets into a position where the future of the Chinese Communist Party itself is at stake Moscow can be counted on to come to its assistance. Unlikely as it appears to be at present, the reverse would also be true. Moscow and Peking are playing dangerous politics with each other, and this increases the potential irrational element in their relations with the West.

The Sino-Soviet conflict has an influence on the psychological-political forces at work in Asia. It gives to Peking somewhat more of the stature of an independent nation-state than it had during the days of "leaning to one side." The Red Chinese claim to represent Chinese nationalism and to be correcting the humiliations of the past, and their expectation, therefore, of the loyalty of the overseas Chinese is all the more plausible. It is that much harder for many to remember the Communist element in this captive nationalism. In fact, one of the important side benefits to Peking of the conflict with Moscow is its appeal to Chinese on Taiwan and abroad.

The prevalence of the view that Chinese foreign policy can be interpreted entirely in terms of nationalism and great state interests is evident in the diplomacy of France, the general willingness to trade with Peking, and the rising pressures to admit her to the United Nations. It is more difficult to get our allies to agree with our general line of avoiding those actions which would tend to strengthen Communist China's position or contribute to the realization of its expansionist goals. This spurious nationalism also reveals the shortcomings of the political policies of the National Government, which—on the grounds that it could not be less nationalist than Peking—has not opposed the conquest of Tibet or the general treatment of minorities by Peking.

We have seen how many Chinese analysts in this country consciously or unconsciously support Peking against Moscow. The impact of the Peking position on Taiwan must be watched very carefully. Others will speak of Japan, but it is obvious that the conflict helps the Chinese with the Japanese, whose long-standing fear of Russia is still a factor in their foreign policy,

There are further consequences of the Sino-Soviet conflict for the United States in the fields of trade and foreign aid. Peking's trade outside the bloc has increased during the last few years, much of it because wheat purchases have increased. Peking buys wheat and sells rice—a good bargain. But imports of capital goods from the West have also increased. The myth of China's great trading potential is encouraged, and the pressures on the United States to give up its embargo have correspondingly increased. The record suggests that China trades for her own profit but also in the hope of using trade for political advantage (as with Japan).

The Sino-Soviet conflict takes the form of interbloc competition in foreign aid, but this does not lessen the competition which both countries promote with U.S. foreign aid. The case for U.S. attention to every possible way in which to expand the world market, maintain Western-style international economic institutions, and assist in sound economic development is stronger, not weaker, as a consequence of the reckless extension of Chinese efforts in Africa, Latin America, and southeast Asia. Our methods may be due for review but not our political objectives. The Sino-Soviet conflict has disturbed but not destroyed the image that the Communist powers have cultivated of the superiority of their methods of economic and political fulfillment.

This is no time to relax our efforts. The pressures which China and the Soviet Union are putting on the underdeveloped countries of southeast Asia are all the greater because of the success of U.S. policies in some other parts of Asia. We should remind ourselves that Japan is prosperous in large part because of the successful policies of the occupation, especially the land reform, which helped to revitalize industry and rob the Communists of a rural base. Taiwan is economically far ahead of the mainland also in part because of successful land reform. The Republic of the Philippines has far to go but has avoided one Communist takeover and is well on the way to constructing a free economy. Largely owing to enlightened British policies, Malaya finally crushed a Communist-led civil war and came to terms with Singapore to set up Malaysia. There is ample evidence, in other words, that where the Western style of economic development is adopted, especially on the land, the contrast with the Communist style is vastly to our advantage.

The Sino-Soviet conflict has shown that mainland China is not, by itself, a great power. It ranks low in naval and air power, and much of its large army is necessary to keep its own people in order. The only weapons it has to use in international affairs are subversion, a powerful enough weapon, and organizational infighting within Communist parties abroad. Unlike the Soviet Union, China is too poor to cover the mailed fist with a velvet glove; but China does not face the military and economic might of the West. She can take advantage of her opportunities, which are in the weak and disorganized societies of the world, because she does not have the responsibilities that go with great power.

The Sino-Soviet conflict, then, makes no fundamental difference to the U.S. position in Asia, because we still have to deal with the bloc as a whole. Peking and Moscow still have fundamental interests in common which, in a real crisis, would outweigh their differences. In the meantime the conflict will complicate the resolution of problems such as Vietnam in a way that was not true of Korea and will possibly increase the difficulties of negotiation. It is well to keep things in perspective: we are paying a great deal of attention to China, but there is the risk that in concentrating on the rift we may neglect the effective unity of the Communist bloc and think of Peking and Moscow as two distinct antagonistic and utterly separate powers—which they are not.

4. U.S. Policy toward the Communist World

—*GEORGE F. KENNAN*

Moscow is faced today with Chinese pressures of the heaviest possible sort which not only demand an immediate deterioration in Russia's relations with the West but obviously have as their concealed aim the provocation of actual hostilities between Russia and the West at the earliest possible moment.

The Soviet leaders are well aware of this. They understand its dangers. They propose, I am sure, to resist these pressures to the best of their ability. But there is one area of world affairs where they are extremely vulnerable, where the Chinese have important tactical advantages, and where the Soviet leaders can be and are being pressed constantly into positions and actions that compromise their relations—with the United States in particular. This is the area of the so-called anti-imperialist movement.

What is involved here is the question of leadership among the various anti-Western and anti-American political forces now competing for ascendancy in the newer or less developed countries of Asia, Africa, and Latin America. To the extent that these conflicts, these so-called anti-imperialist struggles, are highlighted before world opinion; to the extent that they engage the attention of the great powers and become theaters and testing grounds of great power rivalries; to the extent that it becomes impossible for the Soviet Union to ignore or remain aloof from them, Moscow sees no choice but to come down strongly on the anti-Western side, even at the cost of damage to its relations with leading Western countries.

Communism's Only Future

One may well ask why this should be so: what importance do these new countries have for Moscow that could justify so costly a reaction? I can give only a partial answer, because I myself believe this reaction to be exaggerated, oversensitive, and not fully warranted even by the political self-interest of the Soviet regime. Nevertheless, to a certain extent one can see and understand, if not approve, its rationale.

In Europe and North America, the Communist movement as a dynamic, advancing political force is dead. If it has a future anywhere, it is in the developing areas and particularly in the new states where firm political traditions and institutions have not yet formed. Here the possibilities, from Moscow's standpoint, lie less in the prospect of creating real Communist systems (for this, the prerequisites are lacking) than in the possibility of dominant influences being exerted from some Communist center over these inexperienced regimes—of their being developed as instruments of major Communist policy in the game of international policies.

Moscow believes—Moscow is almost obliged by doctrinal conviction to believe—that these anti-Western forces, euphemistically referred to as the anti-imperialist ones, are bound to be generally successful politically on the local scene, at least in the struggle against Western influences. Noting the fumbling, ineffective quality of our own response, I think they have some reason for this belief, insofar as it is we Americans who are primarily involved at the Western end.

The great question, in their view, is: which Communist center is to preside over these various victories and to reap the various fruits? To abandon this field of political contest, or even to neglect it, means, as they see it, to present it on a silver platter to the Chinese. For this, they are not prepared.

Dangerous Indifference

Soviet foreign relations operate in three great areas: the world Communist movement, the underdeveloped and new nations, and the Western world. In the Communist movement, their position is already under heavy and effective Chinese attack. Their relations with the West, while valuable to them, cannot at this historical juncture be expected to carry the entire burden of their international position. A Soviet foreign policy based exclusively on relations with the West would practically undermine the rationale for the maintenance of Soviet power in Russia itself.

Aside, therefore, from the fact that they regard the governments of the new nations as their natural and traditional clients, the Soviet leaders cannot afford, for wider reasons, to stand aside from the struggle for predominance over them. Any such passivity could easily be made to look like indifference to the prospering of the Communist cause generally and would at once be exploited by the Chinese as a means of discrediting Soviet policy and completing the destruction of Moscow's influence and leadership in the world Communist movement.

Beyond that, it would risk the loss of access to this entire theater of international politics, where a continued Soviet presence could alone make the difference between effective Soviet participation in world affairs and a total and ruinous isolation.

In summary, then, the Soviet leadership is a regime subject to strong compulsions toward better relations with the West, yet conscious of having an extremely sensitive flank in Asia and Africa which it can protect only at the expense of its relations with the West. The Soviets walk a very narrow tightrope among these conflicting pressures: vacillating, weaving this way and that, responsive to the shifts in the world scene. Soviet behavior, for this reason, is in part the product of the way we ourselves play our hand and is, in this sense, susceptible in some degree to our influence.

The Alternatives

Two possibilities now present themselves. One is that our relationship with Moscow deteriorates: that Moscow, as a consequence, finds it necessary to hold more closely to Peking in order to compensate for the loss of its Western card; that Moscow then throws itself even more frantically and, having little to lose, even more recklessly and wholeheartedly, into the anti-imperialist struggle—heedless of the effect on Soviet-American relations. Moscow would come to regard as its major objective not the preservation of an effective balance between the Chinese and ourselves as factors in Russia's external situation but rather the successful competition with the Chinese for leadership in the political struggle for our destruction.

This alternative would not satisfy in all respects Chinese desiderata, for the Chinese-Soviet rivalry would continue to be operable in many forms. But it represents in general the direction in which the Chinese, as well as many neo-Stalinists in the Soviet Union, would like to see Soviet policy move.

It would militate for increased unity throughout the Communist bloc as well as for sharper and more uncompromising tactics toward the West. It would compound the effectiveness of the forces marshaled against us. It is difficult to see what ultimate conclusion it could have other than a world war.

The other possibility is, of course, a continued improvement of Russia's relations with us. This possibility would strengthen the hands of both powers with relation to the Chinese: the Russian hand, because the value of the Soviet alternative to the acceptance of Chinese pressures would be enhanced; our own hand, because the intensity of the forces ranged against us would be reduced and because Soviet interests might even work in many ways to reinforce our own position.

In drawing the picture of these alternatives, I should like to avoid the impression that they are absolutes. There is nothing I can conceive of, short of a world war, which could throw the Russians entirely into the Chinese camp. Conversely, any improvement in Russia's relations with the West should not be expected to go so far as to produce any total break with Peking. These are tendencies rather than finalities, but they are tendencies of great importance. And the fact that neither would be likely to be carried to a point of absolute finality does not obviate the enormous significance that attaches to the choice between them.

Peking's Direction

We should recall at this point that the present unhappy state of our relations with China, hopelessly anchored as it appears to be in the circumstances of the moment, should not and must not be regarded as a final and permanent state of affairs. The Chinese are one of the world's great peoples, intelligent and industrious, endowed with enormous civilizing power and with formidable talents, cultural and otherwise. It is wholly unnatural that the relations between such a people and our own should be as they are today.

Dismal as the immediate prospects may be, we must look forward to the day when we come to terms in some way with the prevailing political forces on the Chinese mainland. This, however, like any other adjustment of international relations, will take bargaining and compromise. And if the final relationship is to be a sound one and to bear weight, both sides must have a reasonable bargaining power when they finally sit down to accommodate their differences.

Only if the Soviet Union is kept in the running as an independent force in world affairs, enjoying and valuing a constructive relationship with the West and thus not being solely dependent on the Chinese connection and not helpless in the face of Chinese demands—only if these conditions prevail will we have a chance of working out our long-term relation to China on a basis reasonably satisfactory to ourselves. A well-ordered relationship with Moscow is, in other words, essential to the constructive and healthy adjustment of our long-term relations with China.

If, in place of the preservation and encouragement of Russia's independent role, we force the Russians back into a closer relation with the Chinese—or even into an intense and exclusive competition with the Chinese for leadership in the destruction of our world position—

we will not only intensify the effectiveness of the forces ranged against us at this particular moment but we will complicate greatly (and not to our own advantage) the problem of the eventual composition of our differences with both the Russians and the Chinese.

Basis for Accommodation

If this view be accepted, it becomes an urgent requirement of American policy to ease in every proper and constructive way the relation between the Soviet Union and the United States. This has nothing to do with fatuous one-sided concessions designed to win gratitude on the Soviet side. As one of my Foreign Service colleagues used to say, you can't bank good will in Moscow, and I would be the last to advocate anything of that sort.

But what we can do is to hold out to Moscow a plausible prospect of accommodation in those issues that are theoretically susceptible of solution in this way and avoid the accenting of those that are not. This, as I see it, means serious effort on our part to provide a reasonable basis for accommodation in the great issues of Germany and of nuclear weapons control—in those issues, in other words, that affect primarily the European theater and are central problems in Russia's relation with the West. At the same time, our effort should deemphasize wherever possible conflicts that fall under the Communist category of the anti-imperialist struggle—conflicts in the face of which Moscow, when its hand is forced, is bound to come down formally on the anti-American, if not the pro-Chinese, side.

It does not appear to me that American policy of recent years stacks up very well in relation to this requirement. I have not seen the evidence that we have done all we could do to find agreement with the Soviet Union in matters of Germany and disarmament.

Needless irritations, such as the captive nations resolution and various antiquated trade restrictions, are still permitted to impede the development of Soviet-American relations. Our present involvement in Vietnam is a classic example of the sort of situation we ought to avoid if we do not wish to provoke in Moscow precisely those reactions that are most adverse to our interests. It is largely as a consequence of these strategic errors that we find ourselves in the dangerous and unpromising position we occupy today.

It will be asked, of course, particularly in connection with the problem we now have on our hands in Vietnam, what else we could do than what we have done in situations of this sort.

I would be the last to generalize about such situations or to suggest that a hands-off policy is everywhere possible and desirable. But there is one thing we might usefully bear in mind: the surest way to invite a strong and effective Communist involvement in situations of this nature is to involve ourselves heavily, particularly in a military way.

Where we lay off, the road may be open, ostensibly, to Communist intrigue and penetration. (It is usually open, no matter what we do.) And there may well be takeovers by political forces that make a pretense of Marxist conviction and look to Moscow or Peking for economic aid and political support. But this is not always so intolerable to our interests as we commonly suppose.

The less we are in the picture, the less there is any excuse for actual military intervention on the part of the Communist powers and the greater are the chances for rivalry between Moscow and Peking for political predominance in the region concerned. But in the absence of a Communist military presence and where this Chinese-Soviet rivalry exists, the local regimes—whether nominally Communist or otherwise—are almost bound to begin to act independently in many ways: to develop, in other words, Titoist tendencies. And this is not always the worst solution from our standpoint. It is harder for either Moscow or Peking to interfere extensively with a regime that calls itself Communist than with one that does not. Since we have not engaged our prestige extensively, the situation affords to the Communist powers no such opportunities for political gains at our expense as those the Chinese and North Vietnamese Communists are now reaping in Vietnam.

I can think of nothing we need more at this stage than a readiness to relax: not to worry so much about these remote countries scattered across the southern crescent, to let them go their own way; not to regard their fate as our exclusive responsibility; to wait for them to come to us rather than fussing continually over them. The more we exert ourselves to protect them from communism, the less exertion they are going to undertake themselves.

5. Crossroads of U.S. Asian Policy

—*ROGER HILSMAN*

Our fate and the fate of much of the world may well turn on events in Asia, and our policy is now at a crossroads as momentous as any in our history.

The issue is both political and strategic, and it concerns a long and ominous shadow cast over the whole of the great arc of Asia from Japan and Korea in the north to the subcontinent of India and Pakistan in the south—a shadow cast by Communist China, a nation of 700 million people and continental size whose energies and resources are directed by a ruthless, ambitious leadership.

Today Communist China and the United States are on a collision course. The outcome can only be war.

Indeed, in the present situation the questions are only when the war will come and under what circumstances—whether it will come in ten or fifteen years and be fought with nuclear weapons; whether it will be fought in the next year or two in the limited areas of southeast Asia as a bloody, hand-to-hand struggle against the awesome mass of Chinese manpower; or whether it will be fought in the next year or two in a wider arena and on a larger scale, in which case the question will turn on the use of "battlefield" nuclear weapons and the role of the Soviet Union. And what makes the whole issue so foreboding is that no matter how wise and restrained the United States makes its policies, the ambitions of the Chinese Communists may be so great that they will still insist on a showdown.

U.S. Policy Goals in Asia

Stepping back from this grave and urgent threat for a moment, let us consider our long-range goals in Asia. The United States is today carrying a crushing burden of responsibility in Asia, a burden it probably cannot continue to carry indefinitely. Thus, in the long run, U.S. policy should be to withdraw—but only in the sense of gradually turning over more and more of these responsibilities to peace-loving, stable nations whose governments are responsive to their own people and have no ambitions toward their neighbors. One can visualize a powerful Japan in the north and an equally powerful India in the south as the two poles of a framework of security and stability, with Indonesia, the Philippines, and the others playing large and responsible roles as they develop economically and politically. In the meantime, U.S. policy should be, first, to do all it can to hasten the development that will permit these nations to assume more and more responsibility for the security of the region and, second, to maintain the peace and security of the region without which development would not be possible.

Stating such an overall goal is easy. Accomplishing it will require an extraordinary effort of understanding and analysis. It will take both the determination to stand firm under aggression and the willingness to negotiate. And it will require the patience of years of effort.

Communist China is the foremost obstacle to achievement of a stable peace in Asia. What can the United States do? Some of my liberal friends believe that the problem of Chinese Communist aggressiveness can be solved by recognition or by granting them a seat in the United Nations. But I am most skeptical. It seems to me that the attitudes of the Chinese Communist leaders are so deeply implanted and so implacably hostile that it will take a generation, at least, for them to change. These are the men who made the "Long March" of 8,000 miles to the caves of Yenan, who have lived in dogmatic isolation for thirty years, who are Stalinist in the extreme—primitive and aggressive even by Communist standards. A sudden shift in power from the "Long March" veterans to the second echelon of leadership, coupled with dramatic developments in the Sino-Soviet dispute, for example, could conceivably bring about a rapid change in these attitudes. But ordinarily such basic attitudes change only after a lifetime of bumping against the hard realities of the world.

And this conclusion is reinforced by examination of a series of developments already explored in earlier chapters—a series of events that future historians will probably point to as one of the most portentous international political developments of our time: the Sino-Soviet dispute.

U.S. Policy toward Communist China

What should our policy toward Communist China be? In 1957 Secretary Dulles enunciated a policy toward Communist China based on the assumption that communism on the mainland was a "passing phase." The policy that flowed from that assumption was to do everything possible short of war to quicken its passing—rigid opposition in every way. "We owe it to ourselves, our allies, and the Chinese people," Mr. Dulles said, "to contribute to that passing."

In 1963 it was my great privilege to be the spokesman for a different U.S. policy, enunciated in a speech at San Francisco. This policy—based on what we had learned about the Chinese Communist regime in the six years following Mr. Dulles' speech—was that, unfortunate though it may be, the Chinese Communist regime is not a "passing phase." Reviewing the history of failure of the "Great Leap Forward" and the commune program, the speech noted that the mainland economy collapsed but that the regime did not. "Nor was its authority," the speech continued, "effectively challenged." And the basic assumption was inescapable—that "we have no reason to believe that there is a present likelihood that the Communist regime will be overthrown."

From this analysis a different policy inevitably flows, a policy of firmness, flexibility, and dispassion. By firmness we meant firmness in our determination to maintain our strength in Asia; to stand by our commitments to our allies, including our friends on Taiwan; and to deter and meet Chinese Communist aggression. By flexibility we meant a willingness to negotiate, to talk, to maintain, in the words of the speech, an "open door" to a lessening of hostility. And by dispassion we meant a capacity to look at China policy coolly, with the interests of our nation and of humanity in mind and without the blinding emotion that in the past has clouded our analysis of the problem of dealing with China.

The policy is identical to that which President Kennedy followed in dealing with the Soviet missiles in Cuba. His posture was firm, backed with a determination to use the panoply of American strength. But his policy had the flexibility to provide at each stage of the crisis an acceptable way out for the Soviets and later the dispassion that allowed him to negotiate a nuclear test ban treaty without the emotion of past events clouding his vision of what was good for both the United States and the world.

Certain concrete steps can be taken to implement this policy.* If we took these steps—arranging to have the Chinese invited to the arms control talks in Geneva, lifting U.S. travel restrictions, reexamining some of our trade policies, and proceeding to the recognition of Outer Mongolia—there would be no dramatic results. But these steps would at least begin to put political pressure on the Chinese Communists; to get the United States off the hook it is now on; and to help persuade the peoples and nations of Asia that it is not we who are isolating the Chinese Communists but the Chinese Communists themselves through their pariah policies and attitudes.

In addition, these steps might lay the groundwork with the second echelon of Chinese Communist leaders, those who will replace the "Long March" veterans who are coming to the end of their years, so that they understand that the only hope for the Chinese—and for mankind—is in the long run some form of accommodation.

---

*Outlined in a speech in California in November 1964 and before the Subcommittee on the Far East and the Pacific of the Committee on Foreign Affairs, U.S. House of Representatives, March 1965.

President Johnson recently has moved in these directions—by lifting the travel restrictions on medical scientists and by agreeing to an invitation to the Chinese Communists to participate in the Geneva arms control talks. Both moves are a wise beginning to a very long journey.

Any proposals for U.S. policy toward Asia would be incomplete without an analysis of our position in southeast Asia, especially South Vietnam.

I do not think the United States needs or wants to make of southeast Asia a bastion of anticommunism and a base for American power in Asia. Such ambitions, indeed, would lead only to war. The Chinese Communists would undoubtedly make extraordinary sacrifices in blood and treasure to prevent our taking over southeast Asia—and they could exact a very high price—for the Chinese Communists are not a "passing phase": they effectively control the mainland with its vast manpower and resources. At the same time, the Communists can be brought to realize that we will not tolerate their making southeast Asia into a bastion of anti-Westernism and a base for Chinese Communist power. And with the proper orchestration of military, political, and diplomatic instrumentalities, this task of bringing the Chinese to discipline their ambitions could be accomplished at a cost of lives and treasure that most Americans, though saddened at the necessity, would find acceptable—especially when the costs of the possible alternatives are considered.

The goal, then, is southeast Asia for the southeast Asians. This would mean a neutralized buffer zone including Laos, Cambodia, and South Vietnam. It will require a willingness to negotiate and an overall strategy that puts military measures into a political context.

The War in Vietnam

The United States should stay in South Vietnam. I am heartily in favor of the decision to send U.S. ground forces to Vietnam and to give the Vietnamese military and economic support to the extent of our capability.

But beyond that decision I have grave doubts. The South Vietnamese must themselves be able to take whatever credit there is for defeating the guerrilla terrorism they face. If we over-Americanize the struggle in Vietnam, if we get out in front and make of it an American war, then no matter how thoroughly we pulverize the Vietcong the struggle itself will have been lost in a political sense, which is the only permanent form of either victory or defeat in such a situation. Our ground forces should be used to deter the Communist side from escalation, from upping the ante, but they should not take over from the Vietnamese.

In its international political aspects, a strategy that puts military measures into a political context should maintain a posture of responsibility and disciplined restraint, avoiding any escalation or violation of existing agreements.

Judged by these standards, the bombing of North Vietnam, for example, was a mistake. It was a further escalation and violation of the Geneva accords at a time when the United States should have held to a posture of restraint and of preserving as much of the Geneva agreements as possible. In international terms it was bad politics, raising questions in the minds of the in-between world and doubts among our allies, thus increasing the pressure on us for unacceptable concessions toward negotiations. The one surely predictable consequence of bombing the north was that the pressures on the United States for negotiations would become unbearable. And has anyone asked what would have happened if Hanoi had not been stupid and had accepted the Baltimore offer of negotiations before American ground forces were introduced into South Vietnam?

The bombing of North Vietnam, furthermore, put an obstacle in the way of steps furthering the détente with the Soviet Union. It thus strengthened the hand of the Chinese in their dispute with the Soviets and added credibility to the Chinese argument for more belligerent Communist policies. It made it impossible for the Soviet Union to pursue its own national interest, which was to damp down the possibility of war in southeast Asia, and thus made it impossible for the Soviets to put pressure on Hanoi for negotiations.

But above and beyond all these unwelcome consequences, bombing the north was a mistake for the fundamental reason that it could not be effective. Of course, bombing the north hurts the Communists. It makes them put more effort into maintaining the flow of supplies. They must travel at night. They must have repair crews to fill in the holes in the roads. They must stand by to put timber spans across the bridges that are damaged. But all this is not decisive. It just means more effort, principally more manpower, of which the North Vietnamese and their Chinese allies have plenty. This is not World War II in Western Europe. One does not destroy an underdeveloped, essentially barter economy in which most people live in villages, nor does one destroy communications lines that are dirt roads or trails and simple bridges. The only really effective way to choke the infiltration routes is to supplement bombing, which inhibits their making the routes into full-scale truck roads, with anti-Communist guerrillas who ambush, harass, and in effect force the Vietcong to fight their way across Laos.

The North Vietnamese understand all these things. With their memory of earlier American attempts to fight "immaculate wars" in the air and avoid the blood and muck of jungle fighting, Asians think of bombing as a weak response, an attempt to bluff or at most to use force "on the cheap." All-out bombing, of course, might still force the Communists to negotiate; but this has wisely been ruled out as running too high a risk of general war. Limited, measured bombing, on the other hand, can neither appreciably restrict the use of jungle trails for infiltration nor hurt the North Vietnamese economy enough to persuade them to quit—at least so long as they feel they have a good chance of winning the whole of the country. It is only when the Communists become convinced that the Vietcong cannot win in the south that they will abandon their guerrilla aggression.

But fundamental to winning in the south is an understanding that what the South Vietnamese Government and the United States face is not a war in the conventional sense. A war assumes a hostile population. The tragedy is that conventional military measures will soon create a hostile population if one did not exist in the beginning. An effective counterguerrilla program is as much political as it is military. The effort should be to win the allegiance of the population, to give them physical security and protection from terrorism, in the first instance, but also to give them positive benefits and reasons for their allegiance—land reform, credit at fair terms, justice in law, education, medical services. These are all the things in sum that establish the principle, truly revolutionary for Asians, that governments exist for the benefit of the people.

On the military side, an effective counterguerrilla program must avoid the large-scale military operations that bring destruction and hardship to the people. Guerrilla wars are won not with technological gadgetry, but with feet and brains. The best way to fight the guerrilla is to adopt the tactics of the guerrilla—small patrols, ambushes, and constant movement. Artillery and air power must be used with extreme discrimination. For to bomb a village, even though the guerrillas are using it as a base for sniping, will recruit more Vietcong than are killed. Guerrilla wars have been defeated in the past, but only by a strategic concept that subordinates military measures to a political program. This, unfortunately, we have not yet done in South Vietnam. If bombing the north has been a bad mistake, bombing the south has been a tragic one: it has worked to alienate the people and thus to make the task of a true victory, a political victory, even more difficult. Of course, we must use air power and artillery in the south. Bombing jungle hideouts and headquarters of the Vietcong has made life difficult for them; however, bombing and shelling should be used only when a friendly force is locked in combat with an enemy away from villages and population centers.

An example of the way not to fight a guerrilla war was the operation in the Duchai Peninsula. The peninsula was sealed off and pounded from the air and by naval gunfire. Then the troops went in on a seek-and-destroy sweep. There were perhaps 1,500 Vietcong on the peninsula and 15,000 villagers. Many of the Vietcong were killed and the rest were finally driven out. But according to the *New York Times,* all five of Duchai's hamlets were reduced to rubble and as many as 600 of the villagers killed before they fled. All this may still be redeemable; but it seems obvious that when the troops departed and the villagers returned to what was left of their homes, the Vietcong recruiters would have much material on which to work.

Here are two conclusions: First, although it may already be too late in South Vietnam, the only possible hope for a politically viable outcome is an effective and sophisticated counterguerrilla program. Second, if we do not develop an effective counterguerrilla program in South Vietnam, we will have ample opportunity to try to develop one later—in Thailand and elsewhere throughout the world. For the Communists and especially the Chinese Communists recognize what the advocates of escalation do not yet recognize: that in all but exceptional circumstances the technique of guerrilla warfare can be successfully met only on its own terms and not by the substitution of greater force.

Negotiations

Beyond an effective counterguerrilla program, what should be next? I am most skeptical of negotiations about Vietnam alone. What can be accomplished by negotiations confined to the question of Vietnam? At one extreme the basis for negotiations is that the Vietcong quit. Leaving your neighbors alone is a good principle when applied to, say, France and Germany; but quite apart from the question of its applicability to the two halves of a divided country, why should the Communists agree to negotiate on that basis when things are so palpably going their way?

At the other extreme, the basis for negotiations would be that we quit. It might be possible that the Communists would cooperate in putting as good a face on our withdrawal as possible and easing our way out—although I am not at all sure that they would be so obliging. Perhaps they thought that to be the object of the exercise in 1954. And—an even more ominous thought—they may be bent on humiliating the United States as well as winning Vietnam.

But even if the Communists were to cooperate in trying to put as good a face as possible on our departure, I would hope the United States would never take this course. So long as the South Vietnamese themselves continue to want to resist, we must in honor stand beside them.

And the consequences, if we deserted them—no matter how good a face were put on it—would be disastrous. The whole picture in Asia would change complexion. Our friends could no longer trust our word. Even the neutrals who have dared to follow an independent course would have to make their adjustment to Peking. And what some of my liberal friends must understand, as I mentioned before, is that the whole political fabric of assumptions on which the balance of the world is based would change rapidly. Many of those nations who are content with the present context would, if we deserted them, be forced to build nuclear defenses that they are now willing to forego. It would be a very different and terrifying world.

There are, in sum, only two ways in which we may leave Vietnam. One is as the result of an overall negotiation that establishes a belt of neutralized states for all of southeast Asia and at the same time takes long strides toward an accommodation between China and the United States (which is not likely in the immediate future). And the other is if the Vietnamese decide to quit—and even this is not possible in the circumstances in which the United States has made of Vietnam an American war.

Should we escalate still further? So long as the thirty-five to forty-five industrial sites, dams, and powerplants remain intact in the north, the Communists have an incentive to keep their 300,000 regulars at home. The guerrilla warfare in the south was planned and is directed, supplied, and controlled by North Vietnam; and the cadre of officers and enlisted men controlling the Vietcong have been infiltrated from the north.

If we escalate our bombing of the north, the most probable Communist response would be to introduce the 300,000 North Vietnamese regular troops into the fighting—for the North Vietnamese would then have nothing left to lose. What then? There would be nothing left to bomb in the north and no countermeasure open to the United States except introducing 300,000 additional Americans. Again, the most probable Communist response would be to introduce Chinese "peoples army volunteers" in very, very large numbers.

The debate would then be the same as now, but with the word "Peking" substituted for the word "Hanoi" and the word "Moscow" substituted for "Peking." Should we bomb Peking to force the Communists to desist in Vietnam, and if we did, what would Moscow do?

If we arrived at that situation as a result of our taking the initiative in escalating, I have little doubt what Moscow would do: stand with the Chinese, and with nuclear weapons if necessary. If, however, we arrived at that situation from the opposite direction (because an effective counterinsurgency program was beginning to make headway in the south), there would be considerable doubt that the Chinese would be willing even to try escalation as a substitute for a guerrilla victory in the south.

We have now paused part way up a military ladder of escalation. It will be difficult to remain at this half-way point and dangerous to escalate still further. The Administration says that no alternative has been offered. But there is the alternative of turning the whole perspective upside down and of adopting a political ladder—to which military measures are subordinated.

The heart of the struggle in Vietnam is to win the allegiance of the people away from the Vietcong and toward not so much a "government" as a truly Vietnamese nationalism.

In Vietnam we should "deescalate" the struggle, "demilitarize" it, and "de-Americanize" it. American forces should hold the ports and the airfields and serve as a reserve to reinforce the South Vietnamese when necessary. If attacked, they should defend themselves with all the bombs and artillery they need. For the rest, American power should be used mainly to deter the Communists from escalating the fighting. Vietnamese military power, on the other hand, supplemented by discriminate American airpower, should be used partly to keep the regular Vietcong off balance. But their main effort should be to protect the civic-action teams in the ten to fifteen years' effort of protecting the villagers, eliminating Vietcong agents through patient police work, and winning the allegiance of the people.

At the same time, we should push hard on a policy of firmness and flexibility designed to bring about negotiations not just on Vietnam but on the neutralization of the whole of southeast Asia (or, as a beginning, Burma, Laos, Cambodia and South Vietnam). We should also take concrete steps toward an eventual accommodation between Communist China and the United States.

A collision with China may come no matter what we do. But to talk of Communist China as if hostility is immutable raises Chinese fears that the United States is thinking of preemption. And this will indeed make the collision inevitable.

Vietnam is only the opening chapter in what will be a long, long story. If a holocaust is to be avoided, the United States will need not only wisdom but also self-discipline and restraint and the steadiest of steady nerves. It is not possible to conquer nations in the modern world—especially a nation of 700 million—but it is possible to learn to live with them.

6. U.S. Strategic Opportunities

—ADMIRAL ARLEIGH BURKE

How best to deal with the Sino-Soviet dispute represents a question of grand strategy for the United States.

Because the United States confronts both the Soviet Union and Communist China over control of South Vietnam, we may soon be faced with decisions as grave as those which had to be made with respect to Germany, Japan, and Russia prior to and during World War II. Rather than take the pessimistic view—that the United States faces potential disaster in intervening in the fight for control of the area—I would suggest that both the Communist refusal to relinquish expansionist aims in Vietnam and the American determination to thwart them constitutes an opportunity for the United States.

This opportunity stems from the fact that the Vietnam war has forced the Soviet Union and Communist China into choices undesirable from their point of view. Then, too, Vietnam has exacerbated many of their existing policy differences. In the process, North Vietnam has been caught in the middle. Under these circumstances, the United States has the means of, first, clarifying its policies toward all of southeast Asia; and, second, an opportunity to discredit both the Soviet doctrine of wars of national liberation and the Chinese Communist doctrine of people's wars.

The Soviet Union and Détente

For the Soviet Union, our participation in the Vietnam war has raised serious doubts in the Communist world about the Soviet tactic of détente with the West. Communist China, which from the very beginning opposed any relaxation of tension with the West, now can cite Vietnam as an example of Soviet policy gone wrong. However much the Chinese Communist criticisms may annoy the Soviets, and however effective their obstacles to Soviet aid to North Vietnam may be, their overall impact is minor compared to the losses the Soviets would suffer if forced to give up the benefits of the détente with the West.

The Soviets had hoped to gain a windfall from détente. While they have in fact reaped some benefits, many more would have followed had the détente been extended. Détente could stimulate their lagging economic growth. Relief from high conventional military budgets would permit additional resource allocation to non-military requirements, to advanced military and space research, or to maritime power —all of which could be accomplished without a comparable build-up in the West. If convinced of Soviet sincerity, the West might even be persuaded that it was to its advantage to contribute directly to the growth of a "peaceloving" Soviet Union by a radical expansion of trade and credit policies.

From the Soviet point of view, détente was important for more than economic reasons; it was also designed to relax NATO's stance toward the Soviet Union and to increase tension within NATO. Thus the Soviets might be able to accomplish by a soft and indirect approach what direct pressure failed to accomplish. In other words, if blackmail could not splinter NATO, a prolonged détente might. This policy appears to have yielded important dividends.

Equally important, détente would permit the Soviets a freer hand in extending their influence in the underdeveloped areas. Without risking a direct confrontation with the United States and her allies, they could expand support to "national liberation" movements fighting to overthrow established governments. This could be done in an atmosphere of Western acceptance of a nuclear stalemate, on the one hand, and unwillingness to disturb a relatively tranquil status quo on the other hand. Meanwhile, the Soviets would be in a position to increase investment in advanced weapons research (and development), with the hope or even the expectation of achieving a significant breakthrough. Under conditions of détente, a major weapons development might provide sufficient leverage to initiate psychological, diplomatic, and blackmail actions at the very time when the NATO alliance structure would be fragmented. In short, all facets of the détente tactic might have been timed so that a new period of offensive could take place after the Soviets had closed the gap by drawing closer to the strength of the West.

Soviet Support of People's Wars

Given the increased Chinese Communist commitment to Vietnam, the Soviets now must weigh the advantages of détente against the possibility of a series of successful "people's wars." For the Red Chinese, a victory in South Vietnam would represent a means of regaining face from the political and tactical defeats which they have suffered—notably in Africa and in Indonesia—over the last eighteen months. Decisive victory in southeast Asia would increase Red Chinese influence throughout southeast Asia and would tend to legitimize their militant tactical line while discrediting the "softer" Soviet line.

It is clear that the Soviets have a large stake in the outcome of the Vietnam conflict. To assure their continued leadership of the Communist movement and to offset Red Chinese predominance in Asia, the Soviets would demand full credit for assisting the Vietnamese Communists should the United States withdraw without a decisive victory. This would be true regardless of the reasons for withdrawal—whether a broad-based coalition government including Communists could be established in Saigon; whether internal religious, political, or social unrest could be inflamed to a point at which the existing government could be deposed; or whether a negotiated withdrawal of U.S. and allied forces could be achieved—thus paving the way for eventual absorption of South Vietnam into Hanoi's orbit.

The Soviet Dilemma

For Moscow the dilemma is how to prevent the loss of the benefits of détente and at the same time retain prestige with the Communist world with Soviet Vietnamese policy. This dilemma has constricted the range of Soviet action. The Soviets have not yet committed themselves completely and exclusively to either alternative. Obviously this waiting policy is wise from their viewpoint. However, their attempts to anesthetize the West through détente have been counteracted in part at least by their support of Hanoi since it highlights the fact that détente is a tactic and a phase quite different from a real change of Soviet policy objectives. In sum, there are two major disadvantages for the Soviets in the present situation: Soviet support of Hanoi harms détente; yet Soviet lack of support to Hanoi lends fuel to the Red Chinese accusation of revisionism.

Other chapters in the book have made it amply clear that the Chinese Communists expect to assume ultimate leadership of the world Communist movement; that their strategy for realizing these ambitions calls for hegemony over all of southeast Asia; and that Vietnam was to be the model for people's wars throughout the developing areas of Asia, Africa, and Latin America. Their lack of resources (especially a developed nuclear-strike capability) and our intervention in Vietnam make success more difficult over the short term; however, these obstacles do not divert their long-range intentions. All in all, Vietnam has become the major testing ground of their doctrine of people's wars and perhaps of their future power position.

Communication of U.S. Intentions

Given the various possible interactions among Moscow, Peking, Hanoi, and Washington—and the stakes involved—what courses of action should the United States now adopt? The first problem of strategy, after one's objectives have been established, is often one of communication of intent to the enemy. For, after all, war is a conflict of wills. The best strategy avoids bloodshed by convincing the enemy that he cannot win. We should make it perfectly clear to Hanoi and Peking that we intend to prevail in Vietnam: a clear declaration of intent is necessary both to our security and to the security of the South Vietnamese.

This communication was not effected in the earlier days of the conflict when we talked too much of "helping the South Vietnamese to help themselves." Hence, our greatest mistake in the past several years in Vietnam has been that we never really communicated our determination to the Communists. They perhaps even misunderstood our public goals and statements to the extent of believing that we would withdraw after a period of time. Peking and Hanoi always have the events of 1954 in the back of their minds.

Politically, the United States will achieve its goals for South Vietnam if the Vietnamese people are given the chance to develop into a viable society along the pattern they had chosen before the Vietcong interfered. Strategically, the United States must not alter the policies it has espoused since the turn of the century—that aggression in Asia is our concern. This is the reason we fought in the Pacific during World War II, and if it is *right* now to give up our concern for the area bordering the Pacific, it was *wrong* to fight for it at far greater cost of blood and treasure during World War II.

Strategic Importance of Vietnam

Communication involves credibility, and credibility requires action as well as words. The fundamental principle in our strategy vis-à-vis Peking, Moscow, and Hanoi must be to convince them that the United States considers the conflict in Vietnam to have the same kind of global implications as World War II. Of course this is true. The reason we must stop piecemeal local aggression in Vietnam is that it could lead eventually to a third world war—just as the Austrian episode, the Sudetenland, and finally Poland led to World War II.

The longer the war is allowed to continue, the harder it will be for us to convince the Communists that we are going to win; for the war is psychological and political as well as military. Hence, time is our urgent concern; piecemeal commitment and protracted conflict allow the Communists to complicate and compound the struggle psychologically and politically as well as militarily.

For the United States, the Soviet détente tactic would have the danger of inducing euphoria. By the same token, however, adversaries calculate advantages and disadvantages differently. The Soviets apparently believed that the Austrian peace treaty would be a price to pay for offsetting advantages, but it has obviously turned out to the advantage of the free world. The point is that in the cold war there are essential and nonessential concessions. I think we were right in being allied with the Soviets during World War II to defeat Hitler, but we were wrong in permanently building up their strength and in not keeping them out of Berlin.

So it is with détente, albeit a Soviet tactic rather than a Soviet change of objective. We can afford certain aspects of détente with the Soviets if we recognize that Moscow is still the most powerful and therefore the most dangerous Communist power. This then is part of our capability of maneuver with regard to Vietnam and the Sino-Soviet dispute.

Communist China and Vietnam

The question of our strategic options toward Red China is different from that of our options toward the Soviet Union. The Chinese Communists rather than the Soviets have played the preponderant role in Vietnam. While Ho Chi Minh has looked to both for support, geography at least orients him more toward the Chinese than toward the Soviets. In many ways the Chinese Communists have more to gain from a Vietcong victory in Vietnam than do the Soviets. The Soviets might conceivably be able to salvage some benefits from defeat, but the Red Chinese would suffer an enormous setback. For them, Vietnam has been the testing ground or the showcase for Mao and Lin Piao's doctrine. Defeat of the Vietcong without the fall of Hanoi would be a serious blow; defeat of both would be a disaster for them. A double defeat would force Peking to decide whether to engage the United States directly. To preclude such engagement, the

United States must apprise the Red Chinese of the dire consequences of intervention, even piecemeal intervention. Red China, as much as she wants victory in South Vietnam, does not want war with the United States at this time. The real dangers of U.S.–Red Chinese war lie in the chance of Peking's miscalculation of our will or in her belief that she can intervene gradually with impunity—as she did in Korea.

If Peking and Hanoi are made to face military defeat, they will seek victory through negotiation. Failing that they would probably settle for some sort of stalemate which to them would represent a slowdown of the timetable and more emphasis on the political. The United States has repeatedly offered to stop short of victory—in effect to accept a stalemate—and the Asian Communists have consistently rejected such offers. In no instance, however, have American offers to negotiate been made as a clear alternative to military defeat. Our earlier offers to negotiate, though well intentioned, were premature and poorly timed. Even though the United States had greatly increased its aid to South Vietnam and had inflicted some damage on North Vietnam, our willingness—almost overeagerness—to negotiate was interpreted as weakness and indecision.

Conduct of Negotiations

Assume for the moment that the tide of battle turns against the Communists and that sooner or later they will admit it to themselves. What attitude should the United States then take toward negotiations? First, if the Communists are convinced they are losing, we can negotiate. But our negotiations must be based on the premise that the Communists will try to save by diplomacy what they are losing in battle. I learned this as a member of the negotiating team in the Korean war. We must not sacrifice at the conference table what we have won on the battlefield. The Korean experience should have taught the United States that to let up on military pressures while negotiations are in process simply provides the Communists with the opportunity to recoup and to make additional demands. In Vietnam, the bombing pause of early 1966 re-proved the point.

Second, we should approach negotiations with a great deal of caution. If the Communists took an initial attitude of restraint and demanded few conditions for the initiation of "peace talks," they could bargain for a cease-fire and withdrawal of U.S. troops from combat. Once this was done, the Communists could proceed on the assumption that no United States Administration, having accepted both the bid to negotiate and a cease-fire, could, without serious Communist provocation, propose to the United States public a resumption of the fighting.

The Communists could easily refrain from highly provocative actions and demands, but a series of small demands eventually equals a large demand. For example, they might make a series of demands for small force reductions rather than a single demand for removal of American forces. They might demand that other countries be brought in to help restore the Vietnamese economy or agriculture—and at least some of these countries would doubtless be Communist.

There might be overwhelming pressure on the Administration to accept any terms for negotiation, so long as they embodied face-saving clauses such as provision for a coalition government. Brave talk about the rest of southeast Asia would make United States abandonment of South Vietnam through negotiation no less a defeat. Our actions in Laos and Korea have already devalued our talk. No other Asian nation would count on United States promises.

Third, it should be recognized that Hanoi will not negotiate if negotiation means losing face. However, it is not our problem to create a face-saving device for them by making real concessions. Unlike us, they can easily create such a device through their own propaganda. A case in point occurred after the Summit Conference which was broken up by the U-2 incident. Khrushchev, who had previously given an ultimatum on Berlin, returned home from the conference by way of East Berlin. There he warned publicly against the impatience of those Communists who thought they could wait no longer to gain control of all Berlin. Communist leaders can easily reverse or change their positions if they so decide. We have no obligation to set the stage for them, especially by making concessions.

If the United States successfully halts the Communist drive in Vietnam, does this mean that both the Soviet Union and the Chinese People's Republic will give up their doctrine of wars of national liberation and people's wars? Of course not. But, a major offensive having been repulsed, the Communists might again entertain a détente. We would hope that we could use the interim to reconstruct our Asian alliances. Moreover, détente might become attractive to the Chinese Communists if the Soviets achieve a military breakthrough that causes them to adopt a more aggressive stance.

The Continuing Danger

Increased preoccupation with Communist developments in the Far East, dangerous as they are, can divert us from the larger continuing danger of the Soviet Union. We must take the strategic "long view." In some quarters the hope is prevalent that the Soviet threat is receding, that henceforth the main threat will come from Communist China. The drains of South Vietnam upon the military budget, and the evaluation that the United States will deter the Soviet Union without greatly modifying its present strategic posture, have brought forth signs of American willingness to lower its guard against the Soviet Union—or at least willingness to forgo development of weapons systems that would maintain the superiority of the United States vis-à-vis the Soviet Union.

No tendency could be more dangerous over the long haul. As the French discovered when the Germans easily penetrated the supposedly impregnable Maginot defense system, complacency with existing defensive arrangements in the face of an aggressive enemy is an invitation to disaster. For the United States, "assured destruction" capability is the equivalent of the Maginot defense system; satisfaction with its adequacy could bring about the same consequences. The argument that the United States is at the end of the line technologically, that no radical innovations in defensive systems will be found because scientific knowledge has reached a plateau, reinforces the expectation that the Soviets too will stop looking for new weapons. Nothing could be further from the truth. As long as the United States is an obstacle to Soviet Communist ambitions, the Soviets can be expected to devote their energies to removal of the obstacle. Soviet scientific achievement encourages them.

Dollars spent for research should not be the only measure of United

States efforts to ensure its security. Equally important are the direction of research and the will to break through existing frontiers. For example, merely improving the penetration capability of American missiles is not enough, especially when the United States is vulnerable to Soviet attack. Assurances to the contrary, the American capability to limit damage from a Soviet missile attack is almost nil. Certainly this is an area where intensified research efforts could be rewarding.

The argument for United States caution in providing for a missile defense system because of the psychological impact upon the Soviet Union fails to consider the Soviet mind. Equally fallacious is the argument that U.S. development of new weapon systems would force the Soviet Union into an arms race. American military strength does not threaten any nation seeking peaceful development. If it disturbs the Soviet Union it is only because the Soviet Union is seeking domination—not peaceful development. If the Soviets are indeed softening their attitude toward the United States, they have every means of making their changed attitude known. American military power should represent no greater threat to them than it does to the rest of the world.

As for the Chinese Communists, their growing nuclear capability will continue to present risks. The sheer prestige of possessing the capability supports Chinese Communist claims to great-power status and enhances her influence in Asia. Although the Chinese nuclear capability does not now give her great military power, even her token force of crude nuclear weapons is of immense significance in terms of its psychological and political value. Further development of Chinese nuclear capability might encourage Communist China to engage in a general conventional war in Asia—believing that U.S. fear of nuclear retaliation would prevent U.S. violation of the nuclear threshold.

Many feel that the present Chinese Communist leadership will soon be replaced by a younger generation of leaders who will pursue their objectives in a more restrained way. Part of their anticipated restraint will come as a result of the sobering effect of the possession of a nuclear-strike capability and a reevaluation of their concept of war as an instrument of foreign policy. This is wishful thinking.

Others contend that the Chinese Communists are aggressive because the United States has isolated them. But, to the extent that Communist China is isolated, it is isolated because of her own aggressive actions. Red China has been recognized by a number of nations in spite of her aggression. Thus, isolation is hardly the question. To support recognition of Red China and her admission to the United Nations would be to undermine our security system in Asia. A switch from our current stand would be to undercut the power balance in Asia. It would open the door for an unchallenged takeover of the continent. Should this occur, Japan, Australia, New Zealand, the Philippines, Korea, the Republic of China, Malaysia, and the Indian subcontinent would be brought under increasing pressures. Eventually we—not the Red Chinese—would be isolated in that area.

Our stakes in Vietnam are high. We cannot afford to lose. Defeat would open the door to communism in the East and put us under greater Soviet pressure in the West. Victory would demonstrate the fallacy of the doctrine of people's wars, or national liberation wars; it would strengthen our own determination to resist Communist expansionism whenever it occurs.

Epilogue

Epilogue

—*CLEMENT J. ZABLOCKI*

PREDICTING WHAT WILL TAKE PLACE IN THE SINO-SOVIET DISPUTE IS AT best hazardous. In the past, too many forecasts of communist maneuvers have proved false. One thing is clear: we must watch for the unexpected. For example, when Mao Tse-tung dies, there may be a drastic thaw in the Moscow-Peking freeze, or just as possibly, it may harden even more. Are we really prepared for both eventualities?

When I say "we," I do not mean just the United States. I am referring to the free-world nations. A great deal has been said in the preceding chapters about the break between the Communist powers. Perhaps this has left readers with too much of an impression that tomorrow's history pages will be determined by what happens between Russia and China. Not at all. Our fate, indeed the hope for peace in this decade, depends upon the skill and solidity of free nations in purposeful action of their own. If one disastrous trap lies ahead, it is that we become mesmerized watching the gigantic forces of the other side lock horns while our own unity and resolve disintegrate.

At the risk of drawing too broad a conclusion from all that has so astutely been set down by others, I would say this: Let us take somber warning from the disarray and setback in the Communist camp that has grown out of the Sino-Soviet dispute. All too many ominous signs are now evident that narrow divisions are separating and pulling apart our own ranks. These can swiftly widen into chasms as deep as those within the Communist world. And the consequences can be as bitter and difficult for us. That at the very least is one highly valuable lesson we can draw from the great Red split. If recognized, it may mean that *we,* not they, determine the course of mankind's destiny.

Although the Sino-Soviet conflict has been generally accepted as a true schism for some time, not many years ago there were still some who doubted its seriousness. Indeed, in some quarters there were suggestions that it might even be a hoax to deceive the free world. The seriousness of the conflict, however, was not really questioned by the contributors to this volume. If there is any single consensus in this volume it is that the dispute is indeed quite serious. Thus for the most part the authors who write about the dispute generally, rather than with regard to specific areas, center their discussion on the origin of the struggle and the principal issues and bases of the dispute. At least one observer believes—and this view would probably be supported by many of the other contributors if they addressed themselves to the question—that the formal alliance between the two will continue despite the bitterness of the conflict because the alliance provides some "reinsurance" in the event of a military conflict with the United States.

There would appear to be considerable agreement that the dispute in large measure is a struggle for leadership of the Communist movement by the two giants of communism. In other words, it is in a very large sense seen as what might be termed a jurisdictional dispute, i.e., where is the power center of communism to be located? In Moscow or Peking?

Another conclusion one may reach is that the dispute is a many-faceted one. Some observers tend to place more emphasis on the ideological nature of the conflict than others, but by and large the conflict is seen by all as involving pragmatic as well as psychological, political, historical, and cultural factors. There is much support for the view that differences over tactics and strategy play a major role: for example, differences over the tactics and strategy to be followed in the underdeveloped world, or differences over which area should have priority—Europe *vs.* Asia and Africa, etc.

It is is quite clear that the dispute has had considerable impact on Communist parties all over the world; it has led to splits into Soviet and Chinese factions. In Europe, for example, it has led to greater independence on the part of the local Communist parties. In many instances the dispute has enabled many parties to tailor or think of tailoring their policies more in keeping with the requirements of gaining or maintaining power at the local level (as in Italy, France, and some of the countries of Eastern Europe). In many areas, even when the majority of local party members have sided with the USSR, they have viewed the dispute as beneficial to their own local interests and thus have been reluctant to participate in measures which might lessen the conflict between the USSR and Communist China.

Although it is not always expressed, there would appear to be agreement that the dispute has important implications for United States policy. One author has termed the relationship a triangular one—i.e, the United States, China, and the USSR—in which what one member of the triangle does affects the others. The triangle is perfectly evident in the Vietnamese conflict.

There is no clear consensus on just what U.S. policy vis-à-vis the split should be; it is generally agreed, however, that the United States should not take overt steps to exploit Soviet-Chinese difficulties. Such efforts might well produce effects quite opposite to those intended. Nevertheless, the rift does provide the United States certain significant opportunities in international affairs. For that reason, the United States must watch the dispute closely and do whatever it can to encourage the resultant trends that are consistent with long-range goals of U.S. policy.

Above all, the American people must be aware that we have entered a new world era which will test our ability as a nation to deal intelligently, prudently, and courageously with new—and sometimes unforeseen—problems of political and military strategy. If the past is a harbinger of the future, then I, for one, have no fears. Having demonstrated our ability not only to survive, but also to achieve progress in a bipolar world, we Americans certainly have the moral resources to meet the challenges of whatever international political configurations lie ahead.

NOTES ON CONTRIBUTORS

Editor

CLEMENT J. ZABLOCKI; Congressman, Democrat of Wisconsin's fourth district, Chairman of the Subcommittee on the Far East and the Pacific, and second ranking majority member of the House Committee on Foreign Affairs.

Contributors

ROBERT J. ALEXANDER; former economist with the Board of Economic Warfare and Office of Inter-American Affairs, presently with International Cooperation Administration and professor, Department of Economics, Rutgers University, New Brunswick, New Jersey.

RICHARD V. ALLEN; director, George Washington University Summer Institute on Communism and Democracy, Freedoms Foundation, Valley Forge; research principal and chairman, Studies on Communism, the Center for Strategic Studies, Georgetown University, Washington, D.C.

ADM. ARLEIGH BURKE, U.S.N. (Ret.); former Chief of Naval Operations, presently with the Center for Strategic Studies, Georgetown University, Washington, D.C.; president of the American Ordnance Association; a director of Freedoms Foundation, Valley Forge.

ZBIGNIEW K. BRZEZINSKI; a member of the Policy Planning Council, Department of State, Washington, D.C., consultant to the Rand Corporation, member of the Council on Foreign Relations, New York; director, Research Institute on Communist Affairs; professor of public law and government and member of the Russian Institute, Columbia University, New York, N.Y.

ALVIN J. COTTRELL; former staff member, Weapons Systems Evaluation Group of the Institute for Defense Analysis, presently is political scientist, Strategic Studies Center, Stanford Research Institute; professor, Department of Political Affairs at the National War College, and research principal at the Center for Strategic Studies, Georgetown University, Washington, D.C.

MARIAN A. CZARNECKI; former administrative assistant to Congressman Zablocki, presently the consultant to the Subcommittee on Europe with the Committee on Foreign Affairs, House of Representatives, Washington, D.C.

BERNARD FALL; former professor of political science at the Royal Cambodian Institute of Administration, at present is professor of international relations, Department of Government, Howard University, Washington, D.C.

WILLIAM E. GRIFFITH; former teaching fellow at Harvard University, Cambridge, Massachusetts, and political advisor to the director, Radio Free Europe, Munich, presently a research associate and director of the International Communism Project, Center for International Studies, Massachusetts Institute of Technology, Cambridge, Mass.

A. M. HALPERN; former senior staff member of the Rand Corporation, and faculty member of the Department of Anthropology, University of Chicago, presently research fellow of the Project on the United States and China in World Affairs at the Council of Foreign Relations, New York, N.Y.

ROGER HILSMAN; served as director of the State Department's Bureau of Intelligence and Research, Washington, D.C., and as Assistant Secretary of State for Far Eastern Affairs, presently professor of government, Department of Law and Government, Columbia University, New York, N.Y.

ANNE M. JONAS; former research staff member for the Weapons System Evaluation Division, the Institute for Defense Analysis, at present is political scientist at the Strategic Studies Center, Stanford Research Institute, Washington, D.C.

GEORGE F. KENNAN; former U.S. Ambassador to the Soviet Union, at present is director, National Institute Arts and Letters, and professor, Institute for Advanced Study, Princeton University, Princeton, N.J.

RICHARD LOWENTHAL; former research associate of the Russian Research Center, Harvard University, Cambridge, Mass., senior fellow at the Research Institute on Communist Affairs, Columbia University, New York, N.Y., presently professor of international relations, the Free University of Berlin.

GEORGE A. MARTELLI; former career officer with the British Royal Navy and later served with the British Intelligence, presently is a diplomatic correspondent and African specialist, London.

FRANZ MICHAEL; associate director of the Institute for Sino-Soviet Studies and professor of international affairs, George Washington University, Washington, D.C., formerly director, Far Eastern and Russian Institute, University of Washington, Seattle, Washington.

RICHARD PATTEE; professor, Faculty of Letters, and director of the Department of Modern Languages and Cultures, Laval University, Quebec, Canada, director of the Center of Hispanic Studies, Secretary-Treasurer, Canadian Association of Hispanists.

LUCIAN PYE; senior staff member, Center for International Studies, Massachusetts Institute of Technology, Cambridge, Mass., chairman of the Social Science Research Council's Committee on Comparative Politics, member of Advisory Committee to the director of AID, Washington, D.C.

ROBERT A. SCALAPINO; has served as consultant to the Ford Foundation and to the Rockefeller Foundation, is editor of the Asian Survey, and professor of political science and chairman, Department of Political Science, University of California, Berkeley, Calif.

GEORGE E. TAYLOR; chairman, Department of Far Eastern and Slavic Languages and Literature and director, the Far Eastern and Russian Institute of the University of Washington, Seattle, Wash., appointed to the Board of Foreign Scholarships by President John F. Kennedy.

ALLEN S. WHITING; director, Office of Research and Analysis for the Far East, Department of State, Washington, D.C., member of the Social Science Division, Rand Corporation, former professor of political science, Columbia University, New York, N.Y.

COL. THOMAS W. WOLFE, U.S.A.F. (Ret.); staff member, Rand Corporation, and professor, Institute of Sino-Soviet Studies, George Washington University, Washington, D.C., served as air attaché at the U.S. Embassy, Moscow.

DONALD S. ZAGORIA; senior fellow, Research Institute on Communist Affairs, assistant professor of government, Columbia University, New York, N.Y., member, Social Science Department of the Rand Corporation specializing in Sino-Soviet relations.

Index

PUBLICATIONS of

THE CENTER for STRATEGIC STUDIES

GEORGETOWN UNIVERSITY

National Security: Political, Military, and Economic Strategies in the Decade Ahead, edited by David M. Abshire and Richard V. Allen (New York: Praeger, 1963). 1070 pages.

Soviet Nuclear Strategy: A Critical Appraisal, edited by Robert Dickson Crane (August 1963). A report of the Study Program on Soviet Strategy. 82 pages.

Soviet Materials on Military Strategy: Inventory and Analysis for 1963, edited by Wlodzimierz Onacewicz and Robert Dickson Crane (January 1964). 140 pages.

East-West Trade: Its Strategic Implications, edited by Samuel F. Clabaugh and Richard V. Allen (April 1964). Analysis and inventory of Congressional documents, 1959-1963. 104 pages.

Military Posture: Fourteen Issues before Congress, 1964, edited by James H. McBride and John I. H. Eales (September 1964). 235 pages.

Détente: Cold War Strategies in Transition, edited by Eleanor Lansing Dulles and Robert Dickson Crane (New York: Praeger, 1965). 307 pages.

NATO in Quest of Cohesion, edited by Karl H. Cerny and Henry W. Briefs (New York: Praeger, 1965). 492 pages.

Latin America: Politics, Economics, and Hemispheric Security, edited by Norman A. Bailey (New York: Praeger Special Studies Series, 1965). 313 pages.

SPECIAL REPORT SERIES

Arms Control and Disarmament: The Critical Issues (April 1966).
Dominican Action—1965: Intervention or Cooperation? (July 1966).

Repeated challenges to the strategic interests of the United States demand a continuing identification of critical issues, conflicting views and research information. THE CENTER FOR STRATEGIC STUDIES, Georgetown University, identifies emerging issues, and brings some of them into a constructive confrontation with available research efforts and views of people who draw relevant knowledge from service at top-levels of government, university and business.